Score

Book & Lyrics
by
Richard Nelson

Music & Lyrics
by
Ricky Ian Gordon

Orchestration by Bruce Coughlin

Musical Preparation by E.G. Music Preparation
Musical Supervision by Bruce Pomahac

Original cast recording available on PS Classics Records

ISBN 0-634-08807-6

# VOCAL RANGES OF PRINCIPAL CHARACTERS

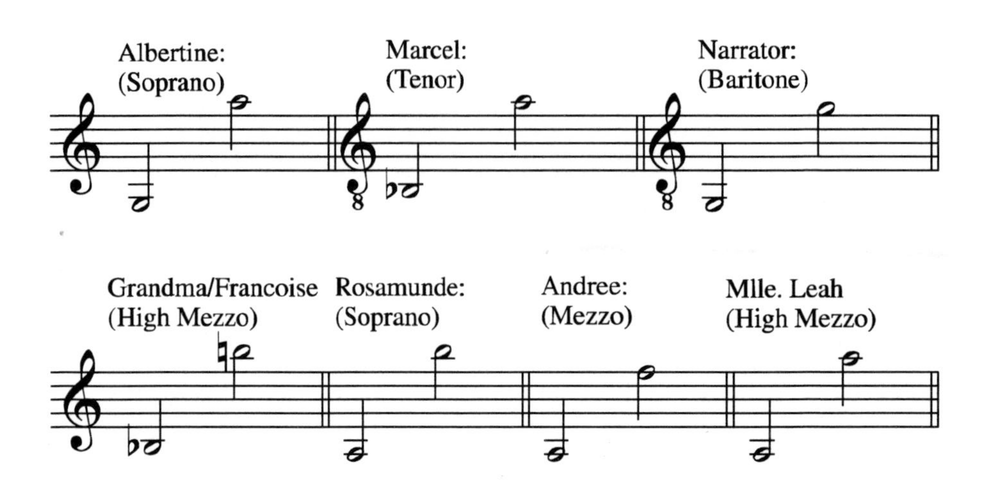


Note: *My Life with Albertine* requires a strong cast of singers. The ensemble is SATB, but they need to be good because the choral work is challenging, bringing the tenor to B♭ and the basses to G. They split up doing various roles—The Stroller, The Messengers, The Bathers. I leave that up to choice, but strongly suggest that a highly proficient group of singers be used for the cast of this show as its challenges are almost operatic.

— *Ricky*

# ORIGINAL PRODUCTION CREDITS

Directed by Richard Nelson
Set Design: Thomas Lynch
Costume Design: Susan Hilferty
Lighting Design: James Ingalls
Sound Design: Scott Lehrer
Music Coordinator: John Miller

# ORIGINAL CAST OF CHARACTERS

| | |
|---|---|
| The Narrator | Brent Carver |
| Marcel | Chad Kimball |
| Albertine | Kelli O'Hara |
| Grandmother/Françoise | Donna Lynne Champlin |
| Mlle. Lea | Emily Skinner |
| Andreé | Caroline McMahon |
| Rosemonde | Brooke Sunny Moriber |
| The Pianist | Paul Anthony McGrane |
| Mlle. Lea's Girlfriend | Laura Woyasz |
| Three Young Men | Nicholas Belton, Jim Poulos & Paul A. Schaefer |

# SETTING

A "salle de theatre" (private theatre in a home), Paris, 1920. A curtained, shallow stage with footlights; to one side, a piano. For much of the play The Narrator (forties) stands by this piano and its pianist and speaks to the audience, telling them about his life with Albertine. The curtain will open to reveal scenes from this life.

# SYNOPSIS

The curtain opens and a young woman (18), Albertine, stands holding a letter. She sings what she has just written ("Is It Too Late?"), a letter asking to be forgiven and taken back. The Narrator tells the audience, "That is the end. I will begin at the beginning... of my life with Albertine."

The first time Marcel met her, he was eighteen, vacationing one summer (1898) at Balbec by the Sea ("Balbec By the Sea"). She was a tough-looking girl unlike anyone he'd ever encountered before, he thought. A polo-cap pulled down over her forehead, she pushed along a bicycle, swinging her hips with confidence. He got himself introduced to her, learned she was actually a middle-class girl who lived with her aunt because her parents were dead. He gets invited to play games with her and her girlfriends ("Oh Ferret of Fairy Wood"). Marcel's Grandmother, with whom he is especially close, interrupts one of these "games," and makes him go to bed. There he cannot sleep, thinking only of young Albertine ("Lullaby"). At the end of that summer, she invites him to visit her in her hotel room. She is alone and in bed. She tries to sing him a passionate poem she has been reading ("My Soul Weeps"); he interrupts, trying to kiss her. She threatens to call for help; he tries again, and she rings for help.

Back in Paris, Marcel's Grandmother dies ("Prayer"). Feeling alone and adrift, Marcel begins to aimlessly attend adult "society" ("A Change in the Weather"), while also trying to write/compose ("Sonata"). Albertine suddenly and surprisingly arrives at his door, looking older and different. Now she allows, even encourages him to kiss her ("The Different Albertines"), and soon she sleeps with him. Marcel then breaks off the affair, having achieved all that he had set out to achieve.

Back at Balbec (reprise) again that summer, he avoids Albertine, ignoring her messages, until one day he and a friend happen into a dingy casino. There they see Albertine dancing with a girlfriend, their breasts touching. Marcel can't stop watching and his friend informs him that it's the nipples of a girl's breasts that get her most aroused ("Tango"). Confused, interested, excited, Marcel invites Albertine to tea at his hotel, where they happen to come across a well-known lesbian couple. Marcel watches Albertine closely to see how interested she is in this couple; he is pleased that she appears not to care at all until he realizes she has been watching them the whole time in a mirror ("Tango" cont'd). He leaves her; she follows him to his room. Lying, he tells her he loves someone else; he tells her he knows about her and her girlfriends; she denies it all. She says she dances with her girlfriends because there are no boys who know how to dance as well. "Could she teach him?" She puts music on the pianola ("Tango" reprise). They dance. She opens his mouth with her tongue. And they become a couple.

The Narrator ends the act by singing "The Song of Solitude" ("on any given day, half the human race is in tears").

# INTERMISSION

Marcel and Albertine and her friends visit a dance hall in Paris where a Female Singer has the stage ("I Want You"). To Marcel's surprise, Albertine knows this singer and is cajoled to sing with her, even sing her own song ("I Need Me a Girl") about loving a girl, which ends in a dance, and Marcel, jealous, takes her home, where he now essentially locks her in his apartment, telling no one (except his servant Francoise) that she is even staying there.

Marcel tries to work (composing at the piano), but is distracted by Albertine as she, naked, heads off to take a bath. The Narrator now joins the story and sings with Marcel a duet about their love/lust for this young girl ("Sometimes"). Albertine's best girlfriend, Andree, whom Marcel is paying to spy on Albertine, arrives and reports on her innocent comings and goings. The Narrator, though, jumps to a future conversation with Andree when he learns (he thinks) that Andree and Albertine are in fact having an affair at this time. Marcel, of course, knows none of this. He allows Andree to go and see Albertine in the bath. From off stage, he and the Narrator hear them sing and play in the bath ("Oh Ferret of Fairy Wood" reprise).

Confused ("A Change in the Weather" reprise) and still trying to compose ("Composing"), Marcel is interrupted by his own thoughts (a chorus of girls singing the sexy "Sometimes" reprise) and decides that he must tell Albertine to leave. But before he can, Francoise enters to say that Mlle Albertine is gone.

Upset and angry, Marcel reads her letter ("Albertine Is Gone/Four Letters") and responds, telling her to go to hell. She writes back saying she'll never forget him, even in the arms of another. He writes that he's going to marry her best friend, Andree, and before this can escalate further, he suddenly scribbles out a telegram begging her to return on any terms. As he calls for Francoise to send the telegram, she arrives with the news that Albertine has fallen off her horse, broken her neck, and is dead.

Francoise then gives Marcel (and the Narrator who has remained an alter-ego in these scenes, talking with Marcel as one talks with oneself) a letter from Albertine that she obviously wrote just before she died. Marcel reads it; in it she asks to be forgiven and allowed to return ("Is It Too Late?" reprise). Curtain.

The Narrator finishes his story, explains how he would never have written anything without Albertine. He then says that there is one song he's written that did not fit anywhere into this story, so he's put it here. He calls Albertine out and she sings the simple, pure, straightforward love song, everything that Marcel and the Narrator have been seeking and never found ("If It Is True"). The end.

# INSTRUMENTATION

## Reed I

(Flute, Clarinet & Alto Sax)

## Reed II

(Clarinet, Bass Clarinet & Soprano Sax)

## Trombone

## Accordion

## Piano

## Percussion

(Snare Drum, Suspended Cymbal, Crash Cymbals, Concert Tom-Toms [high and low], Timpani, Vibraphone, Xylophone, Bells, Glockenspiel, Triangle, Crotales, Mark Tree, Bell Tree, Tambourine [with skin], Tam-Tam, Castanets, Slapstick, Cowbell, Ratchet, Wood Block, and Anvil)

## Violin

## Cello

# COMPOSER NOTE

I was in a reluctant mood the day Charlie Prince brought Richard Nelson to meet me on a hunch that he was making a good match. I was preparing to go out of town for a new production of my show "Only Heaven," for which I was doing a lot of rewriting and orchestrating, as well as trying to finish the second act of "Morning Star," the opera I was working on with William Hoffman for the Lyric Opera of Chicago. I was feeling overwhelmed and disgruntled, and I had heard the name Proust bounced around and thought... well, that I would be buried alive. Then I met Richard, a charming magnetic man who, almost upon meeting him, could convince me to jump out of a plane if need be.

We spoke of his interest in dramatizing the one story of Albertine and Marcel which runs through Proust's "Remembrance of Things Past," and within minutes of listening to his passionate discourse on this, what seemed then, monumental idea, I was hooked. I uttered a tentative "let me think about it" for self protection, and he left with Charlie.

Less than a week later, I received a call. Richard had finished an outline for Act 1 as well as sketches for many songs—lyric ideas, which he suggested I work on with him. I was stunned at how quickly he was working, with, or without me, and I thought, ok, I have to give this a go for him. I went home, and began work on "Is It Too Late?" thinking maybe I would find the language, and if what I came up with seemed natural and Richard liked it, I would just do it. Sometimes you just have to see if you can enter a piece. I was very excited after I wrote that one song. It seemed the subject matter, the place and time, called upon a world of musical influences which seemed easily accessible to me. I was obsessed with the French "Les Six" growing up—Poulenc, Honneger, Tailleferre, Milhaud, Auric, and Durey—as well as the scores for all the French films I loved so much; the films of Truffaut (Delerue, Jaubert), Carne, Chabrol (Jansen), Godard, Resnais (Fusco), Rohmer (though he never used music).

Anyway, it was an easy world for me to enter, and once I started, it seemed to flow very quickly. We continued working that way, Richard giving me ideas and lyric sketches, and me finding music and reconstructing things as well as adding things. The music seemed to be writing itself and consequently, the lyrics took shape quickly as the music and musical moments defined them. I was reading my head off as well—Proust, Proust, Proust. When I went away to Dayton, Ohio, I was waking up at 5:00 every morning, working for two hours on "My Life with Albertine," two hours on "Only Heaven," and two hours on "Morning Star." I was staying next to a very beautiful white cathedral which seemed, with its solemn deep bells, like the church of Combray, and I felt cushioned and supported by the place. Even those bells ended up in our piece. By the time I arrived home a month later, we had Act 1.

Tim Sanford came over with a small entourage from Playwrights Horizons, and heard me sing/screech through it as Richard told the story and read scenes... and Tim asked us to open the new Playwrights Horizons Theater on Theater Row. The music feels to me like, if I put everything I know to be French—the things I mentioned, adding the visuals of Degas, Manet, Monet, Toulouse Lautrec, Picasso, Matisse, Utrillo, and the poetry of people like Verlaine, Rimbaud, Appolinaire, Beaudelaire—and throw it all in the blender, then add a dash of Offenbach and Faure—a melange, so to speak.

Sometimes, interesting things happened in our process together. I remember one day, we had a reading at my apartment when we had a great deal of Act 2. There was a place where Maurice looks out the window as Albertine is going out. Richard wrote a monologue wherein Marcel spoke of the entire world seeming to whisper her name. I knew this should be a musical sequence and soon after, this became "The Street." I remember how hyper and jubilant I was when I called Richard, having found the frame at the end of "If It Is True," the one song which Marcel could not put in his story and had to tack on as a sort of coda. I was so happy to go back to the opening "Albertine" chords and motif. It felt so right and I'm sure I half deafened Richard over the phone that day.

Oh... I want to tell you one other wonderful thing about Richard and our process. Before I ever committed a note or word to paper, Richard did a kind of mock-up, fake "My Life with Albertine" with a tentative outline, using songs and music I had already written, brilliantly archived from my already existing body of work, to kind of give me the feeling that I could do it because I had already done it! This man knows composers!
We had a good, easy collaboration, Richard and I. I felt at all times like I was doing what I was supposed to be doing, and I often called Richard excitedly playing and singing to him over the phone from whatever city I happened to be in. We had a dream cast.

I am forever grateful to Rodgers and Hammerstein/Williamson Music and Hal Leonard Corporation for publishing this score so that hopefully this piece can have a rich future.

# TABLE OF CONTENTS

## Act I



## Act II

# IS IT TOO LATE?
# (Albertine's Last Letter)

Tempo (poco più mosso)
Rit.
+Cym.
+Vibes
Tempo
ALBERTINE:
Is it too late for me to re - turn to you?
8va
+Fl,Vln. (harm.)
+Cl.
loco
+Acc.
+Sus Cym.
Tempo
Would
L.H.
you be pre - pared to take me
Rit.
+Fl,Vln. (harm.)
+Cl.
+Acc.
+Tbn.

Tempo (moving forward)
back?
What -
+Fl.
e - ver you de - cide,
what -
+Fl,Cl,Vln.
+Sus Cym.
Poco rit.
e - ver you de - cide,
I
shall a -
Rit.
bide
by your de -
+Acc.
+Vln.

Tempo
Poco accel.
Rit.
(to 31)
ci - sion.
+Fl,Cl,Stgs. (Trem.)
+Tri.
+Vcl.
+Euph.
Tempo
Rit.
If you know now, I beg, please, don't
8va
+Fl,Vln. (harm.)
+Cl.
loco
+Acc.
+Sus Cym.
Tempo
make me wait.
The
L.H.
+Vibes
Rit.
ink from your pen will seal my
8va
+Fl,Vln. (harm.)
+Acc.
+Cl.
cresc.
+Sus Cym.
+Vcl.
+Euph.

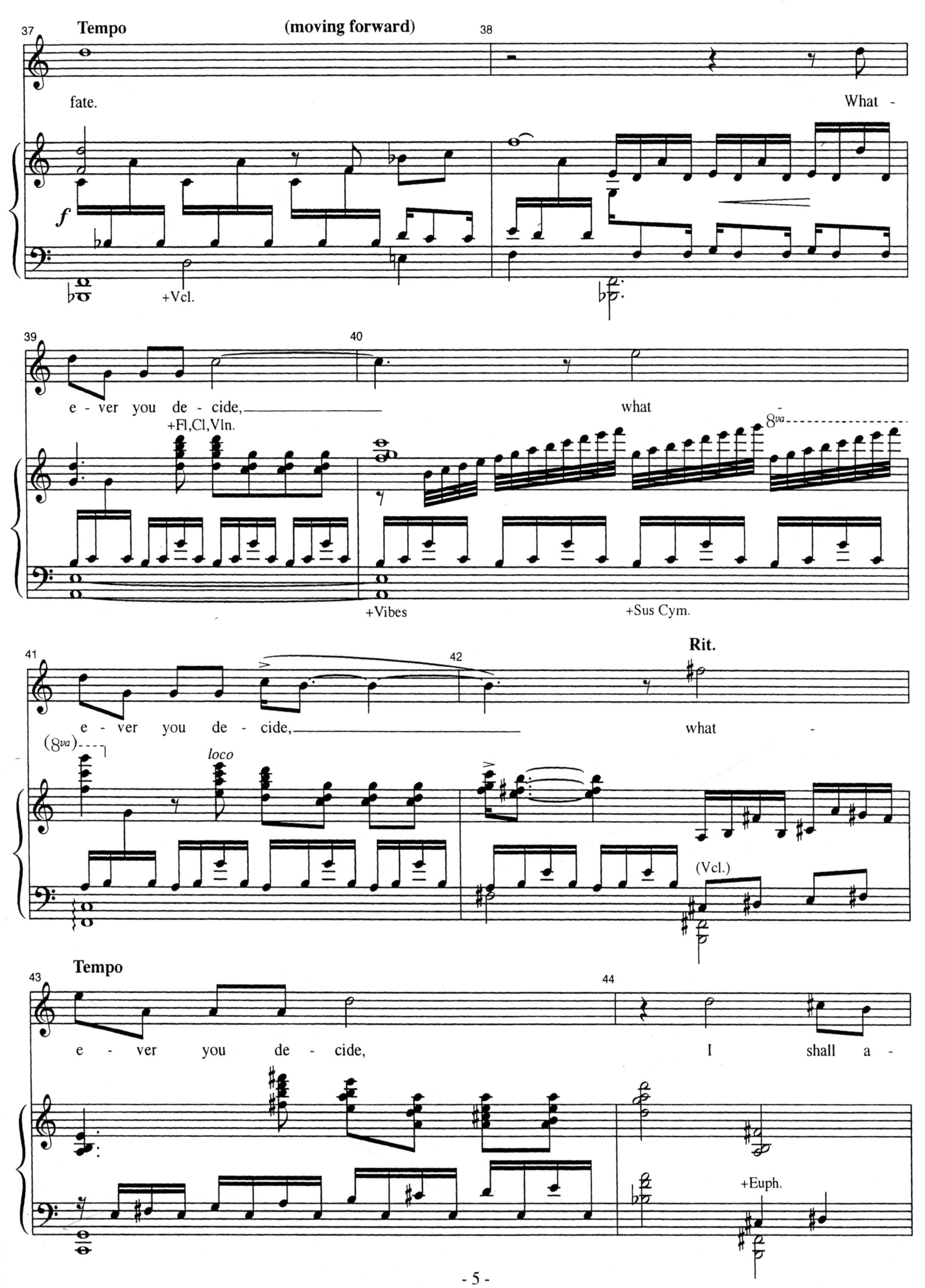

Tempo
(moving forward)
fate.
What -
+Vcl.
e - ver you de - cide,
+Fl,Cl,Vln.
what
+Vibes
+Sus Cym.
Rit.
e - ver you de - cide,
what -
loco
(Vcl.)
Tempo
e - ver you de - cide,
I shall a -
+Euph.

45
Poco accel.
46
Poco rit.
bide by your de - ci - sion.
+Cl.
+Vln. (Trem.)
mp

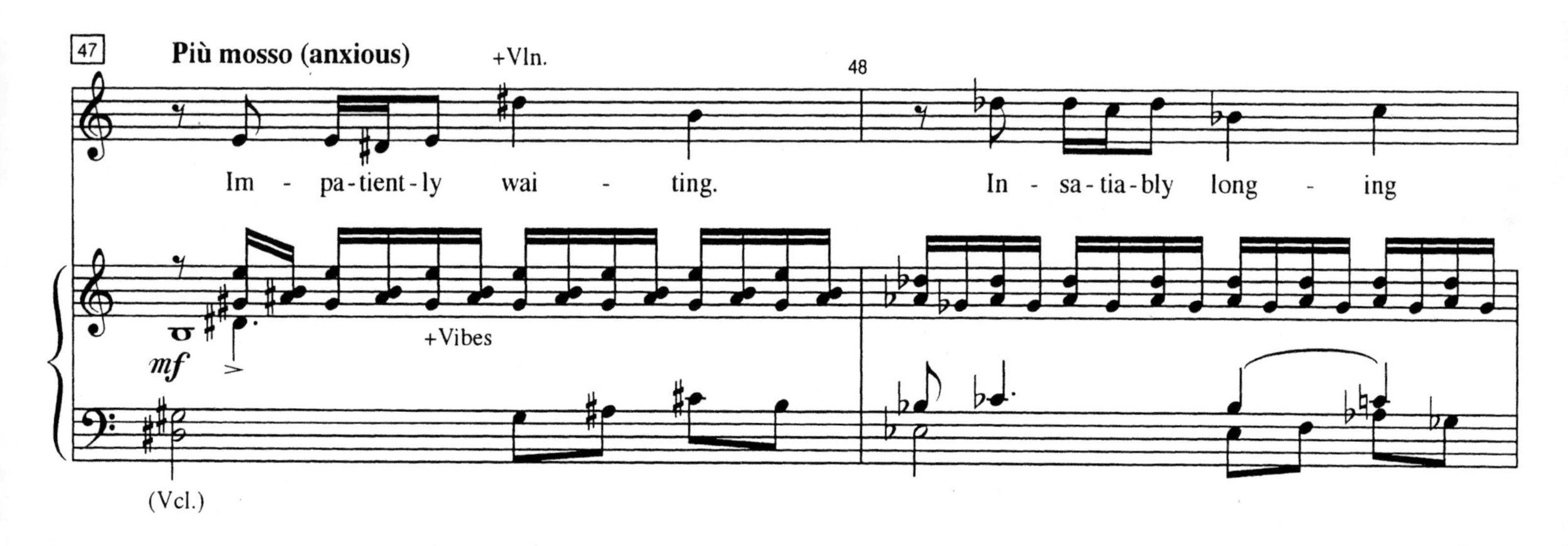
47
Più mosso (anxious)
+Vln.
48
Im - pa-tient-ly wai - ting. In - sa-tia-bly long - ing
mf
+Vibes
(Vcl.)

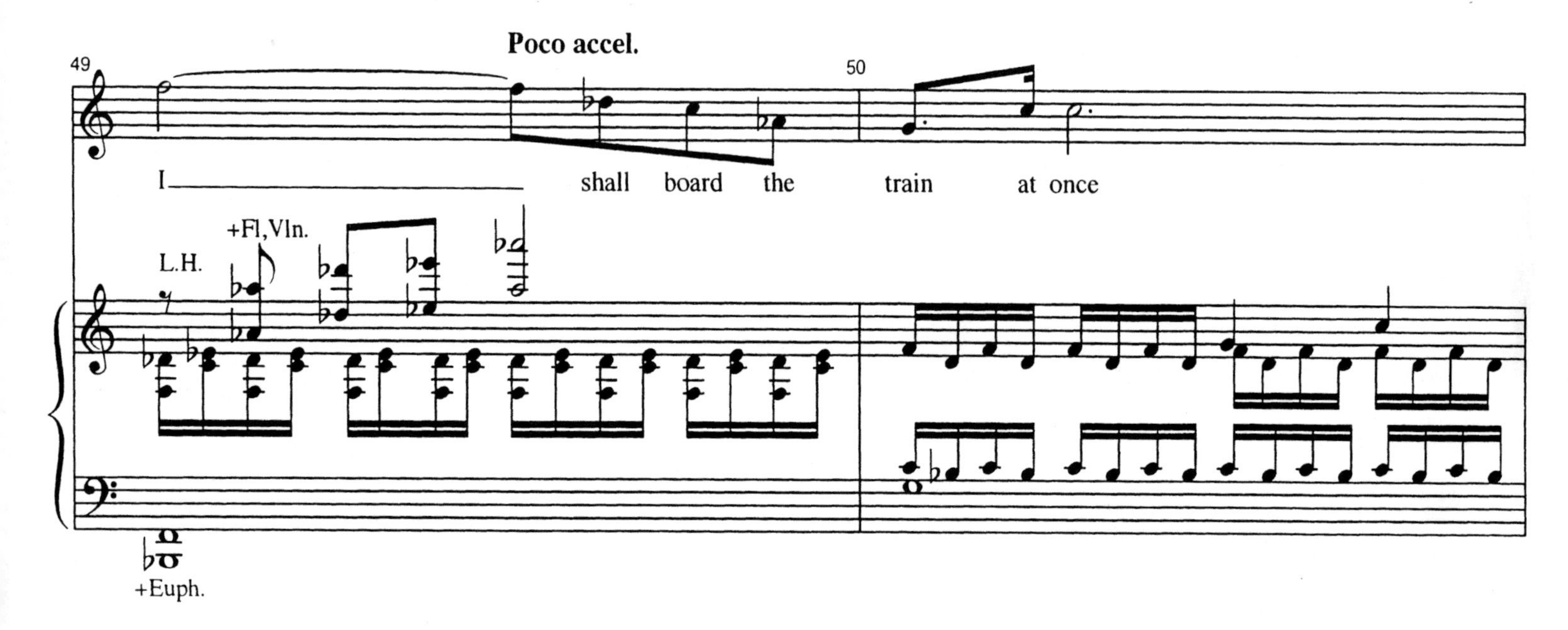
49
Poco accel.
50
I shall board the train at once
+Fl,Vln.
L.H.
+Euph.

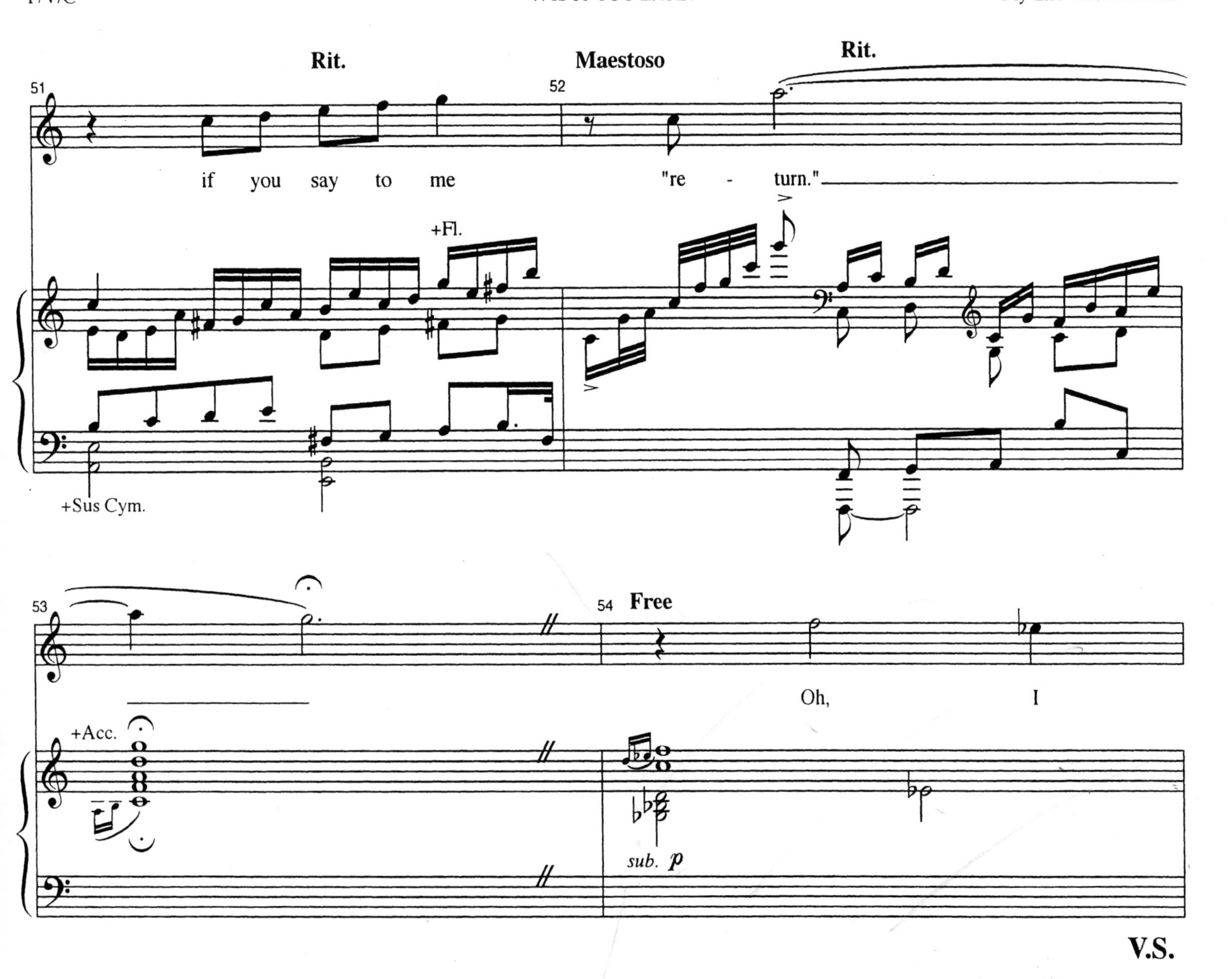
Rit.
Maestoso
Rit.
51
52
if you say to me "re - turn."
+Fl.
+Sus Cym.
53
54
Free
Oh, I
+Acc.
sub. p

V.S.

55
A tempo (meno mosso)
56
Rit.
burn to know..
I
+Fl,Vln. (harm.)
+Cl.
mp
+Acc.
Vcl.
57
Tempo (più mosso)
58
yearn to know
Fl,Vln,Vibes
L.H.
+Vibes
+Cym,Euph.
59
Rit.
60
Tempo
My whole heart is ach - ing.
L.H.
+Cl,Acc,Vln.
+Vcl.
61
Rit.
62
Tempo
My whole heart is yours.
L.H.

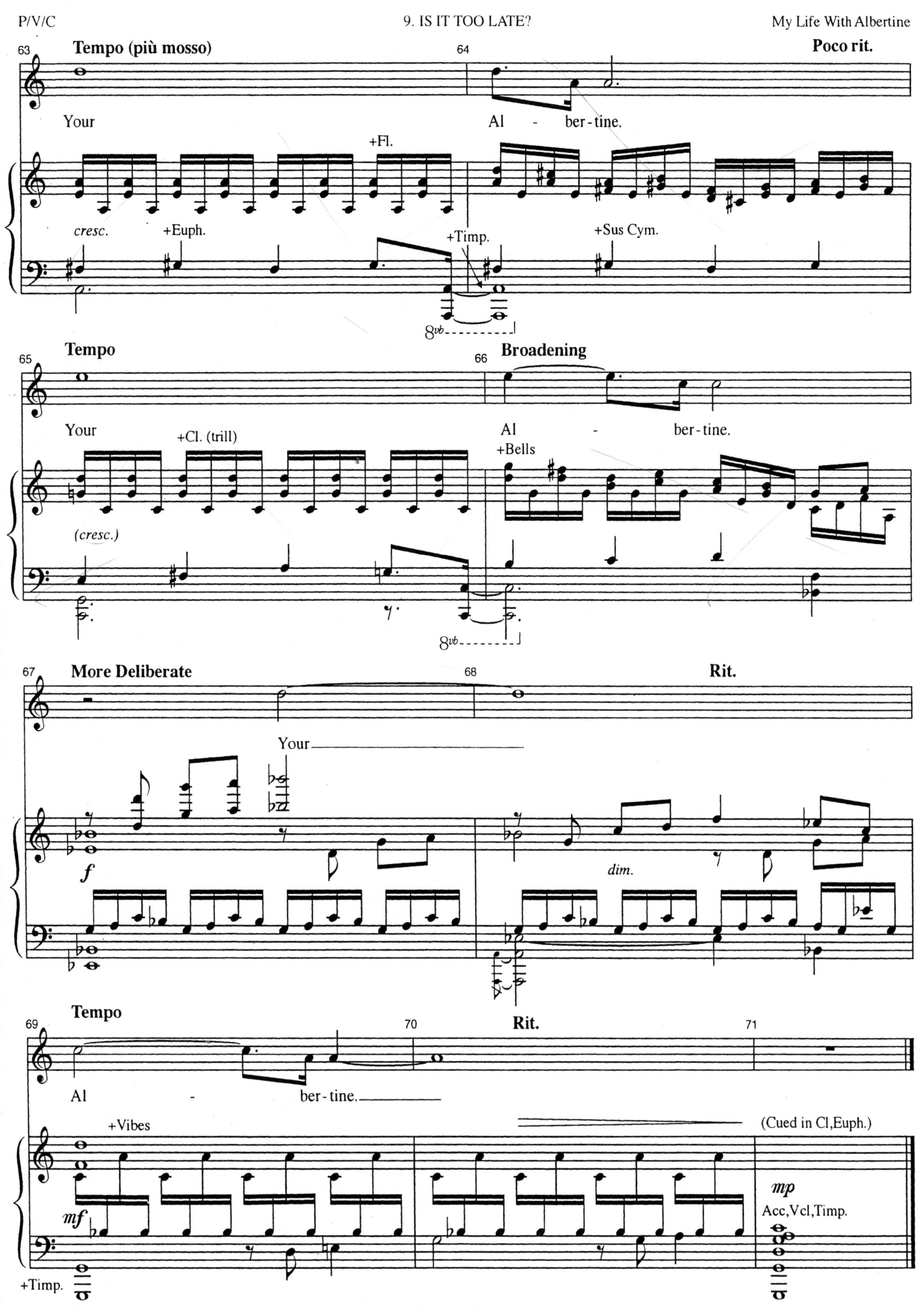
63
Tempo (più mosso)
64
Poco rit.
Your
Al - ber-tine.
+Fl.
cresc.
+Euph.
+Timp.
+Sus Cym.
8vb
65
Tempo
66
Broadening
Your
+Cl. (trill)
Al - ber-tine.
+Bells
(cresc.)
8vb
67
More Deliberate
68
Rit.
Your
f
dim.
69
Tempo
70
Rit.
71
Al - ber-tine.
+Vibes
(Cued in Cl,Euph.)
mf
mp
Acc,Vcl,Timp.
+Timp.

# INTRO TO BALBEC

2nd x: "I caught her..."
Slower ♩ = 80
"a sidelong glance"
+Cl,Acc,Vln
mp
+Vcl.
+Tbn.
"Her name...Albertine."

**Segue as one**

This page left blank intentionally for page turns

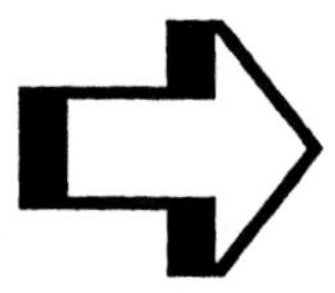

# BALBEC BY THE SEA

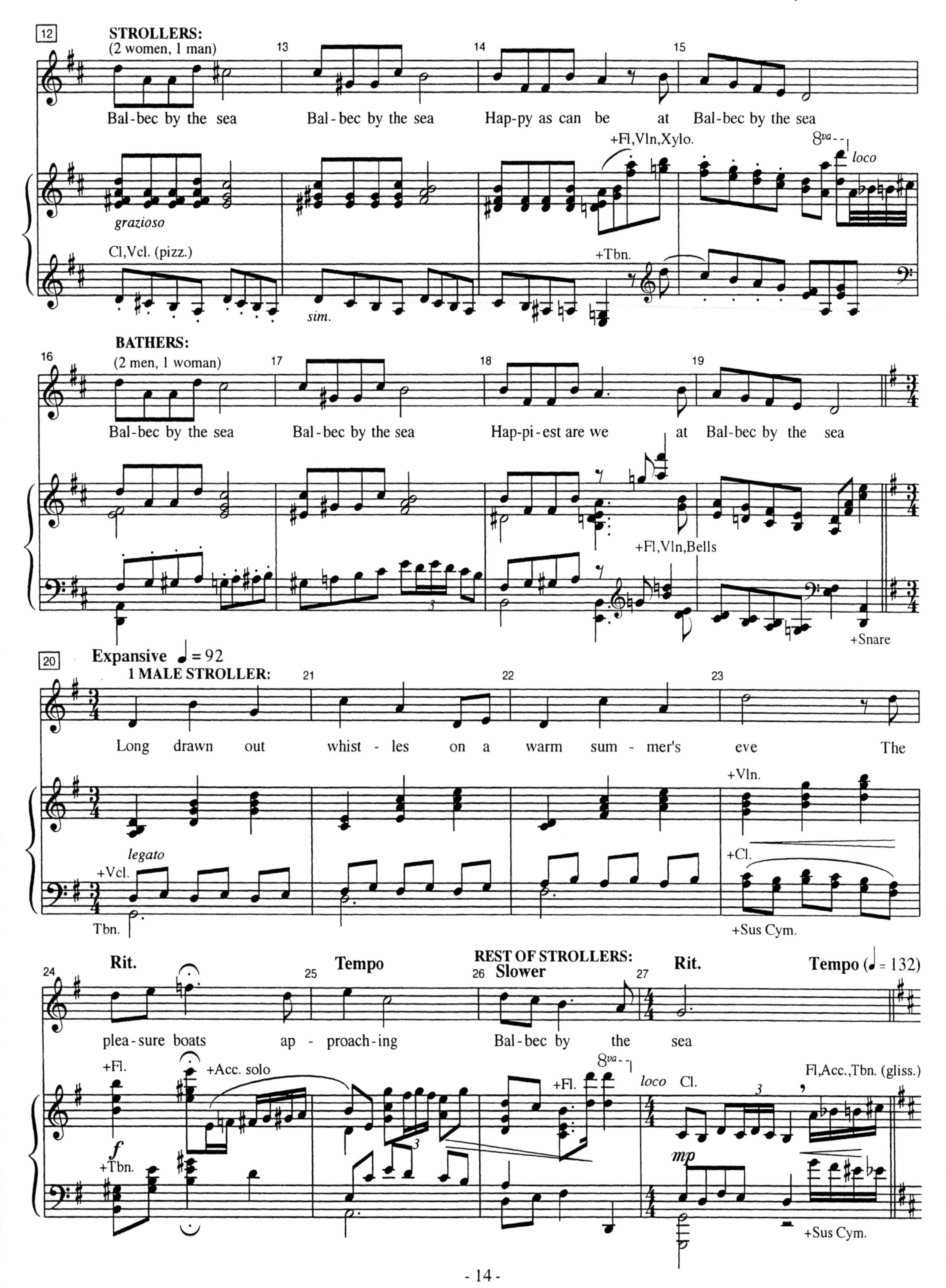
12
STROLLERS:
(2 women, 1 man)
Bal-bec by the sea Bal-bec by the sea Hap-py as can be at Bal-bec by the sea
+Fl,Vln,Xylo.
8va
loco
grazioso
Cl,Vcl. (pizz.)
sim.
+Tbn.
BATHERS:
(2 men, 1 woman)
Bal-bec by the sea Bal-bec by the sea Hap-pi-est are we at Bal-bec by the sea
+Fl,Vln,Bells
+Snare
20
Expansive ♩ = 92
1 MALE STROLLER:
Long drawn out whist - les on a warm sum - mer's eve The
+Vln.
legato
+Vcl.
+Cl.
Tbn.
+Sus Cym.
Rit.
Tempo
REST OF STROLLERS:
Slower
Rit.
Tempo (♩ = 132)
plea-sure boats ap - proach-ing Bal-bec by the sea
+Fl.
+Acc. solo
+Fl.
8va
loco Cl.
Fl,Acc.,Tbn. (gliss.)
f
+Tbn.
mp
+Sus Cym.

28
BATHERS & STROLLERS:
Bal-bec by the sea
Bal-bec by the sea
Hap-pi-est are we
at Bal-bec by thesea
+Vln.
+Fl.
+Fl, Vln, Xylo.
+Cl.
+Vcl. (pizz.)
Tbn
Cl
Tbn.
Cl.
BATHERS & STROLLERS:
Ah Ah Ah Ah Ah Ah at Bal-bec by the sea
Poco rit.
Bal-bec by the sea
Bal-bec by the sea
Hap-py as canbe
at Bal-bec by the sea
+Fl. (trill)
+Bells
+Bell of Cym.
36
Expansive ♩ = 92
SAME MALE STROLLER:
Paint - ed by Whist - ler with an o - pal - like glow called
Poco rit.
+Vln, Fl. solo
+Cl.
mf
legato
+Vcl.
sfz
+Mark Tree (gliss.)

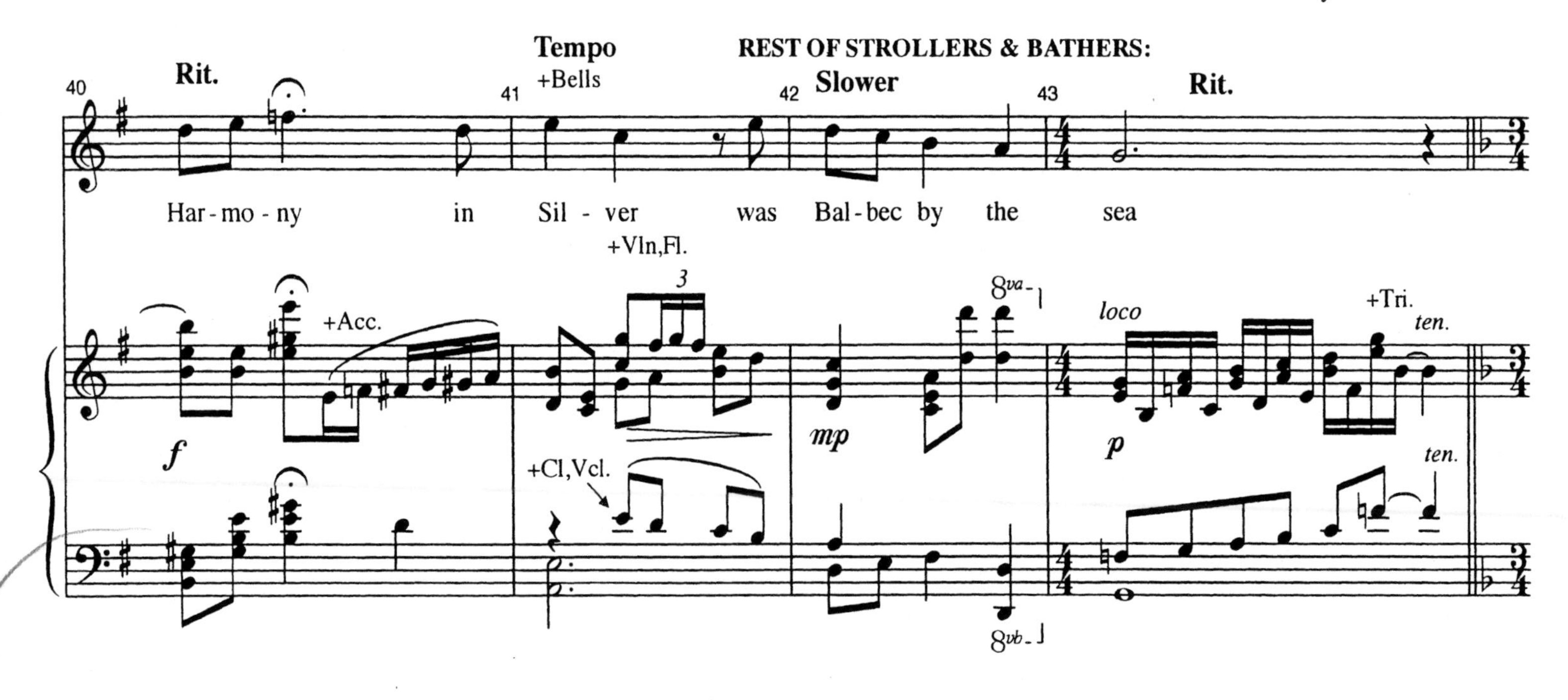
Rit.
Tempo
+Bells
REST OF STROLLERS & BATHERS:
Slower
Rit.
Har - mo - ny in Sil - ver was Bal - bec by the sea
+Vln,Fl.
+Acc.
loco
+Tri.
ten.
+Cl,Vcl.
ten.

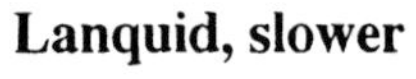
Lanquid, slower

BATHERS & STROLLERS:
Pur - ple light Pur - ple light Blue green un - dul - lat - ing sea
Pur - ple light Pur - ple light Blue green un - dul - lat - ing sea
NARRATOR:
Pur - ple light be - neath a cur - tain Blue green un - dul - lat - ing sea
+Fl.
loco
+Vln. (harm.)
loco
+Tbn.
+Cym. (brush)
+Acc.
loco
loco
+Vcl. (pizz.)

Rit.
Tempo (♩ = 132)
ten.
Out-side con-cert ser - an - ad - ing Bal-bec by the sea
Out-side con-cert ser - an - ad - ing Bal-bec by the Bal - bec by the sea
Out-side con - cert ser - an - ad - ing Bal-bec by the sea
8va
15ma
+Fl.
+Acc.
+Tri.
+Vcl.
8vb

52
Tempo ♩ = 132
BATHERS:
Bal-bec by the sea Bal - bec by the sea Hap-pi-est are we at Bal-bec by the sea
Fl.
+Xylo
Cl,Acc,Vln.
8va
loco
Tbn,Vcl.
+Tbn,Vcl.
+Slapstick

BATHERS & STROLLERS:

56 57 58 59 Poco rit.

Ah— Ah— Ah— Ah— Ah— Ah— at Bal-bec by the sea

Bal-bec by the sea Bal-bec by the sea Hap-py as can be at Bal-bec by the sea

+Fl. (Trill) +Bells

+Bell of Cym.

60 Maestoso (slower) Tempo

ALL (except Marcel): 61 62 MARCEL: 63

Bal-bec by the sea Bal-bec by the sea Ev-'ry morn-ing I would be im - pa-tient to wake up and see

*f* +Vcl. +Fl. *loco* Cl. +Fl. +Acc.

64 Rit. 65 ALL:

which sea would be play-ing just for me at

+Cl,Vln. +Acc. +Vcl. +Tbn. +Bell of Cym.

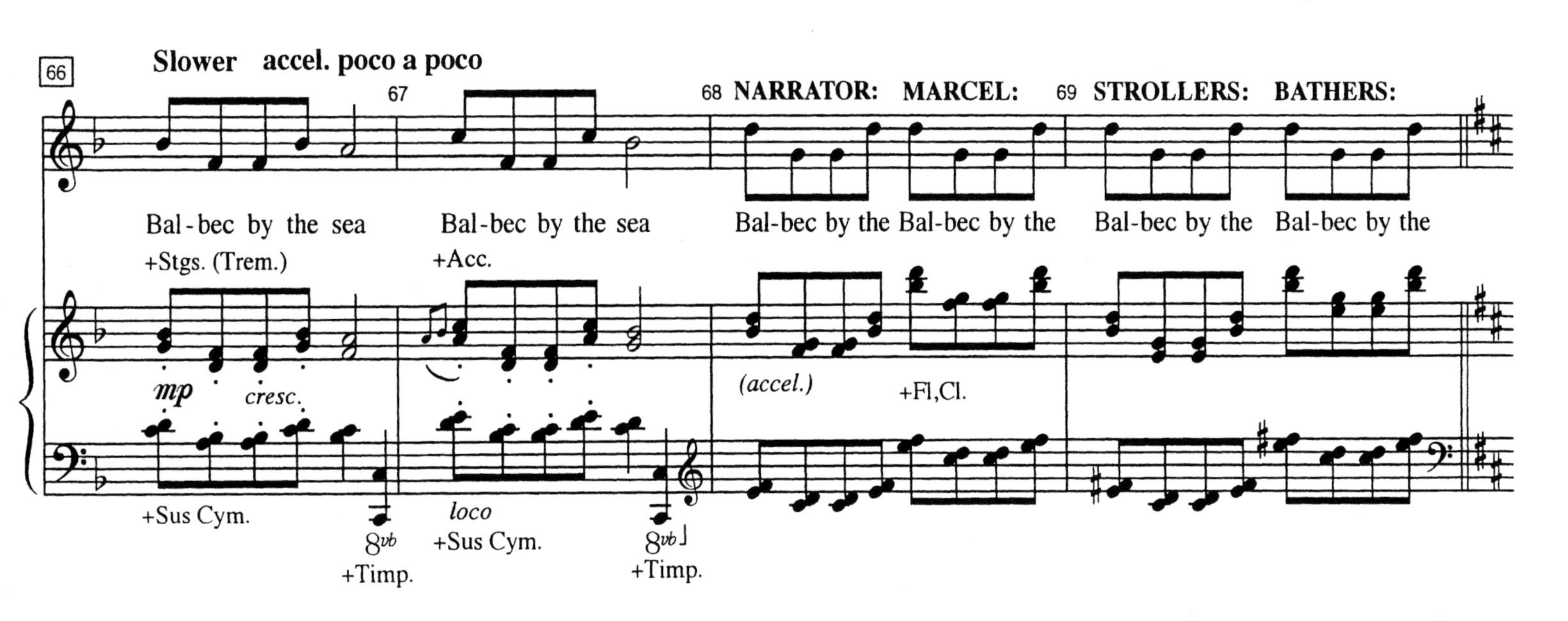
Slower accel. poco a poco
NARRATOR: MARCEL: STROLLERS: BATHERS:
Bal-bec by the sea Bal-bec by the sea Bal-bec by the Bal-bec by the Bal-bec by the Bal-bec by the
+Stgs. (Trem.)
+Acc.
mp cresc.
(accel.)
+Fl,Cl.
+Sus Cym.
loco
+Sus Cym.
+Timp.
+Timp.

Tempo
ALL:
Poco rit.
Bal-bec by the sea Bal-bec by the sea at Bal-bec by the sea
MARCEL/NARRATOR:
MARCEL:
MARCEL/NARRATOR:
Bal-bec by the sea Bal-bec by the sea On my grand-ma's knee at Bal-bec by the sea
Fl,Vln.
Cl.
+Fl.
+Cl.
+Fl,Bells
+Tbn.
+Vcl.
+Tbn.

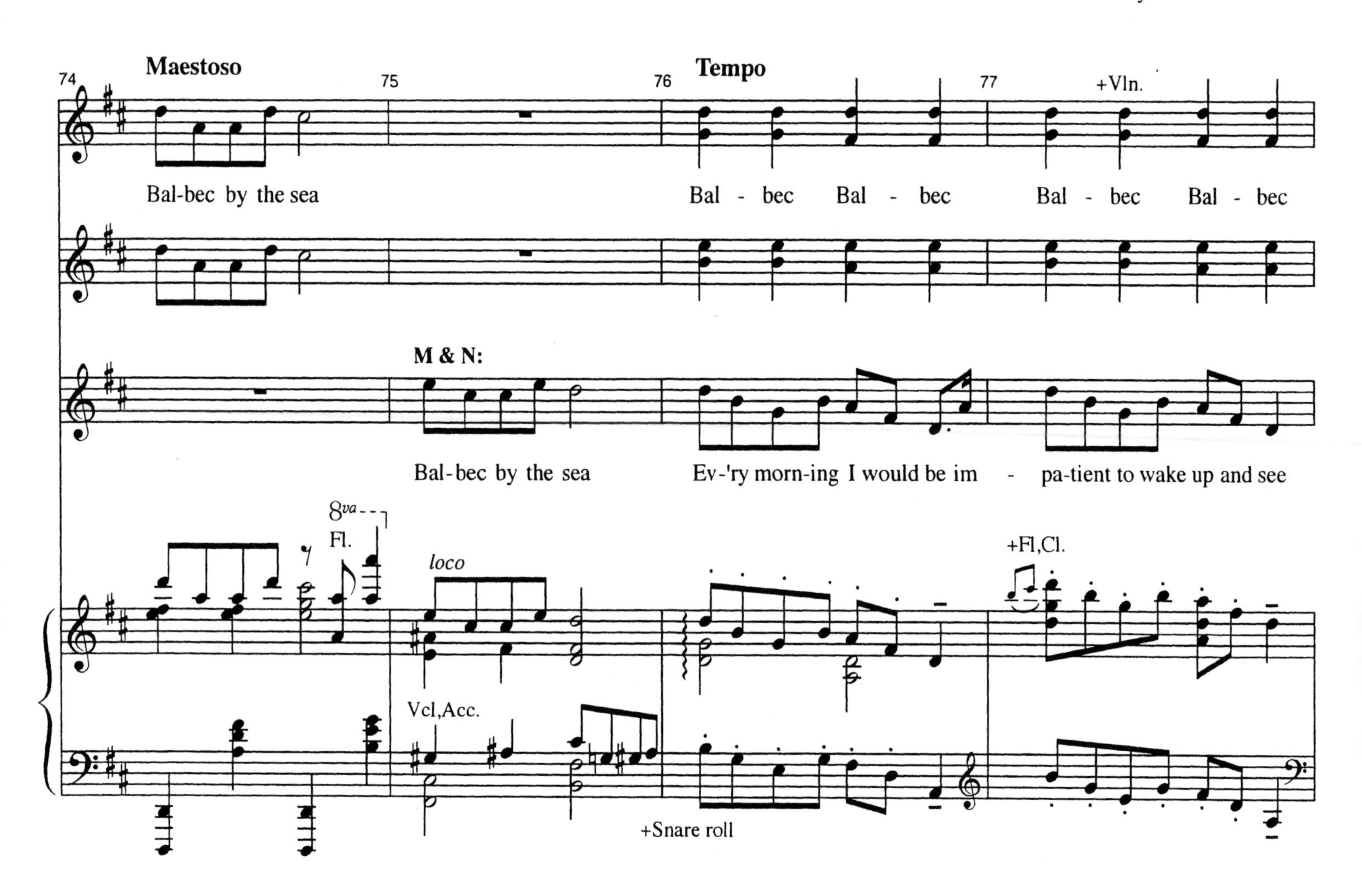
Maestoso
Tempo
+Vln.
Bal-bec by the sea
Bal - bec Bal - bec Bal - bec Bal - bec
M & N:
Bal-bec by the sea
Ev-'ry morn-ing I would be im - pa-tient to wake up and see
8va
Fl.
loco
+Fl,Cl.
Vcl,Acc.
+Snare roll

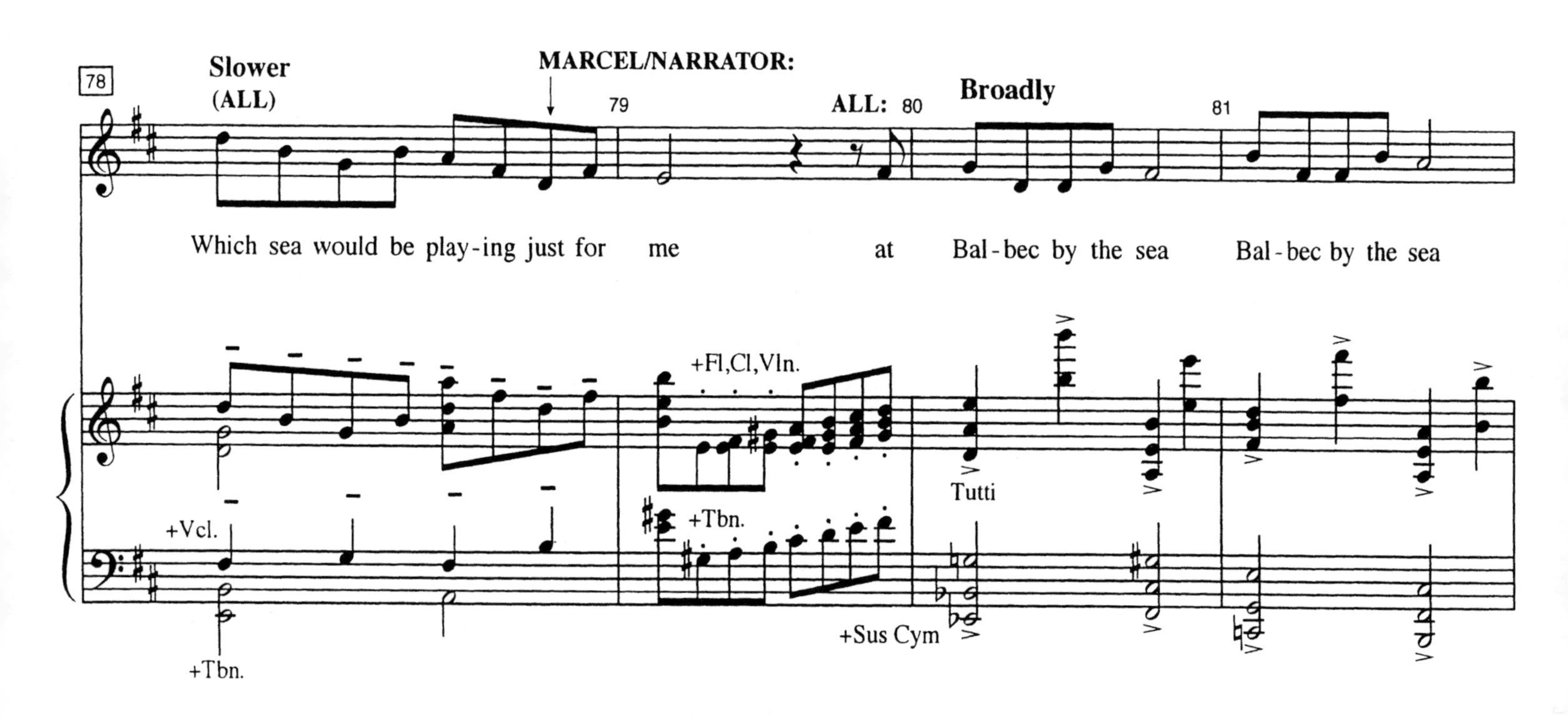
Slower
(ALL)
MARCEL/NARRATOR:
ALL:
Broadly
Which sea would be play-ing just for me at Bal-bec by the sea Bal-bec by the sea
+Fl,Cl,Vln.
Tutti
+Vcl.
+Tbn.
+Sus Cym
+Tbn.

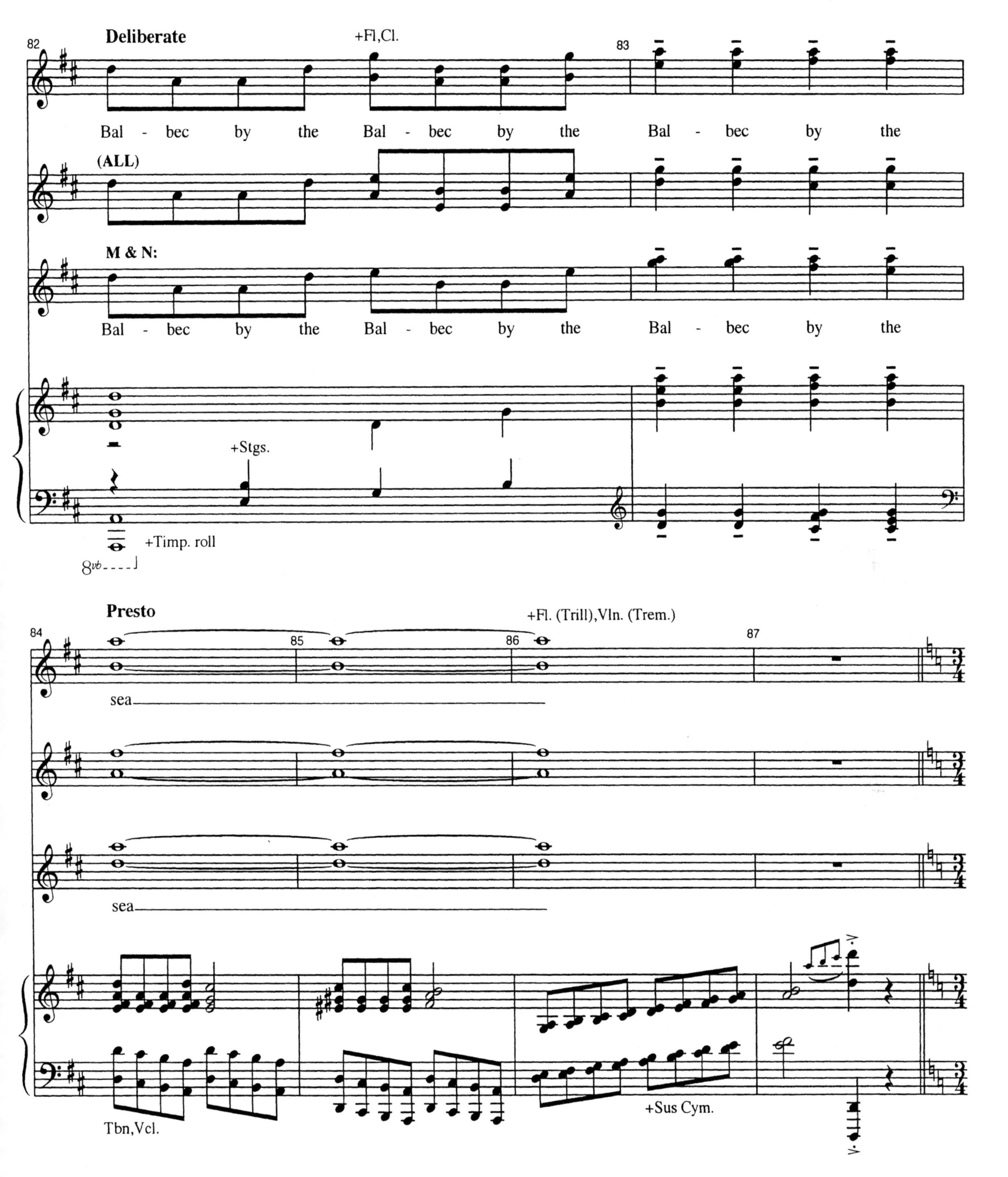


V.S. to PLAYOFF

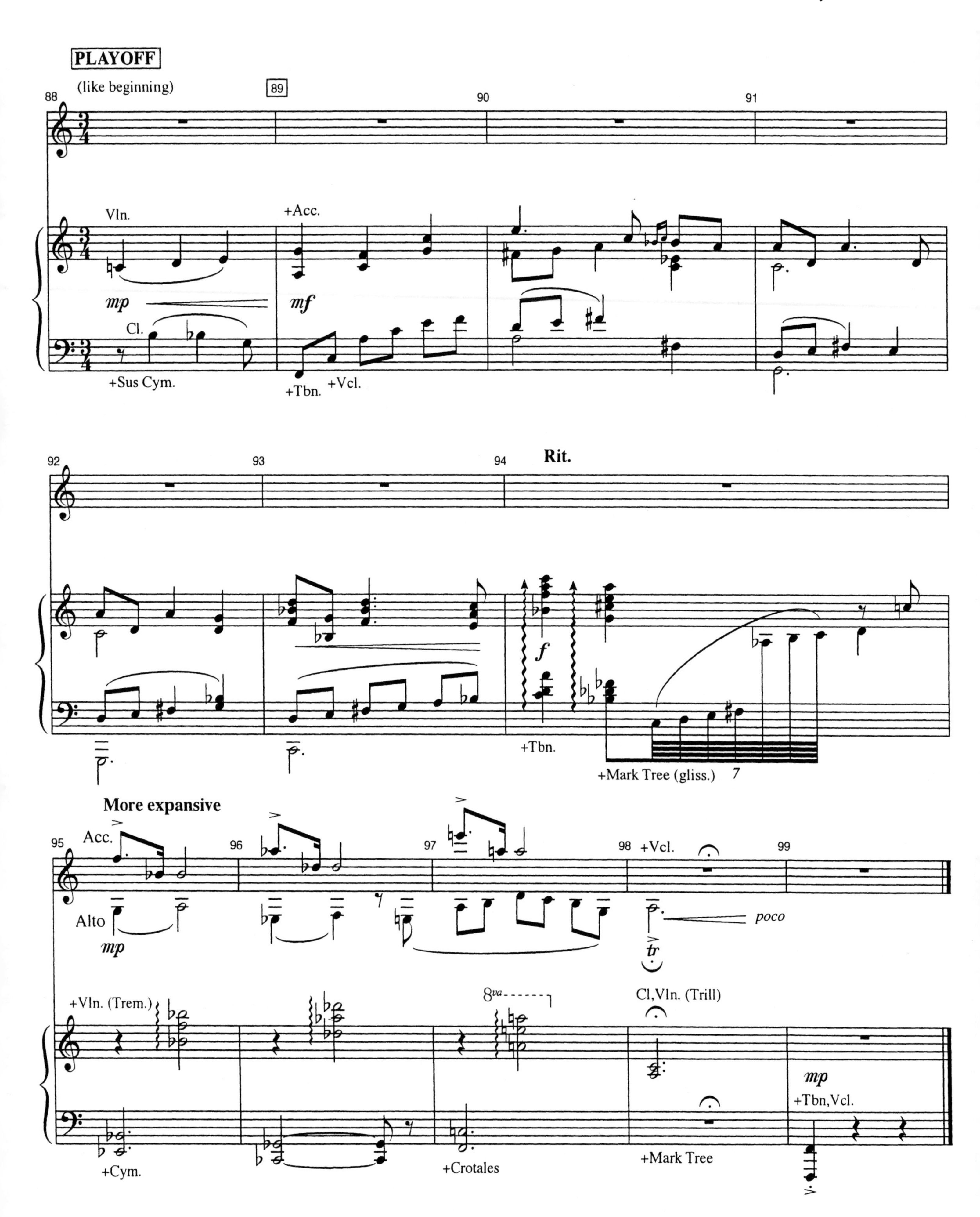
PLAYOFF
(like beginning)
89
Vln.
+Acc.
mp
mf
Cl.
+Sus Cym.
+Tbn.
+Vcl.
Rit.
f
+Tbn.
+Mark Tree (gliss.)
7
More expansive
Acc.
Alto
mp
+Vcl.
poco
tr
+Vln. (Trem.)
8va
Cl,Vln. (Trill)
mp
+Tbn,Vcl.
+Cym.
+Crotales
+Mark Tree

# BARCAROLLE UNDERSCORE

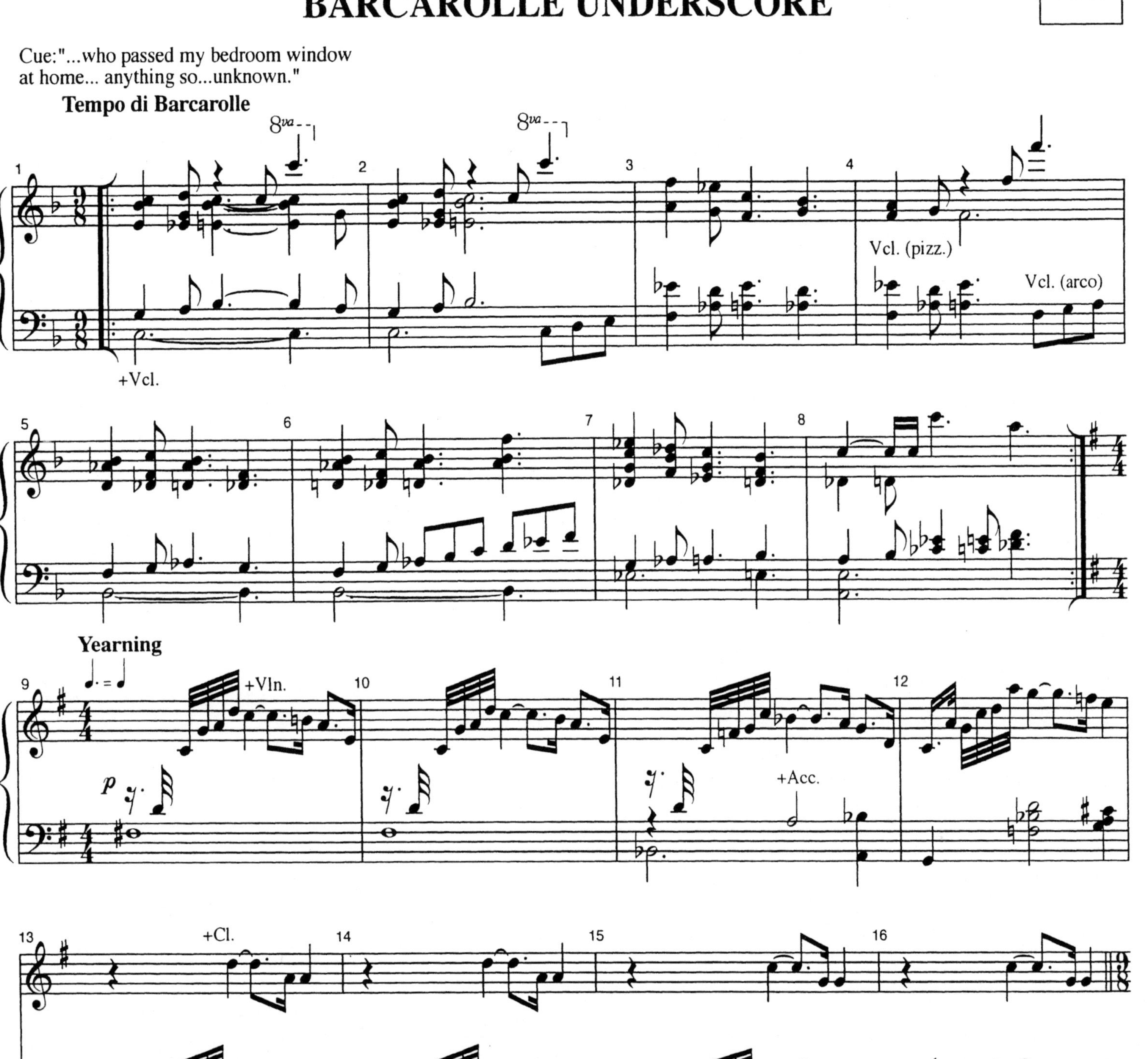


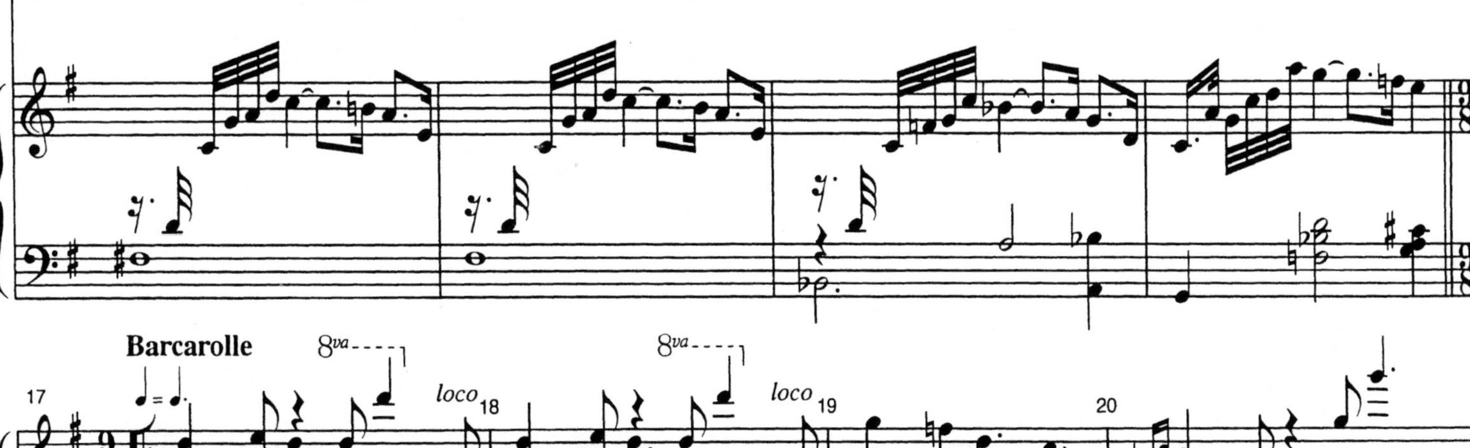

+Vln.
8va
Yearning
+Acc.
Jump on cue
"...babe at the breast"
+Cl.
+Acc.
+Vln.
+Cl.
Segue as one

# LULLABY

Segue from No. 2a

Tempo
Sleep
Sleep
Do not think why
Lul-la-by
+ Fl, Bells
+ Stgs
+ Cl
cresc.
+ Acc
Poco rit.
(optional cut to Bar 44)
my child
Lul - la-by
(Stgs)
+ Fl
(cresc.)
+ Sus Cym roll
Vcl
Slightly faster
Lul - la - by in the gar - den where dream flow - ers grow
Vln
+ Fl, Cl
Vln
Acc, Vcl
Vcl
+ Euph
+ Euph
Rit.
Tempo
Lul - la - by my child of a world we'll ne - ver
+ Fl, Cl
Vln (trem)
Vln
Euph

Rit.
28
Tempo I°
know
Fl, Vln
8va
loco
+ Sus Cym
Vcl
Acc
Dream
Fl, Cl, Vln
mp
Vcl (pizz)
Dream
In pas - tures lie
Lul-la - by
loco
8va
Vln loco
Cl, Vcl
+ Euph
Rit.
Tempo
my child
Lul-la - by
+ Fl
Vln
Acc
Vibes
Vcl
+ Acc
Sleep
Sleep
Soft
Vln
+ Fl, Bells
Vln, Vcl
+ Cl

Accel. poco a poco
clouds drift by
Lul-la-by
Vln, Vcl
Cl
+ Sus Cym roll
cresc.
+ Euph, Acc
Rit.
my child
Lul-la-by
Vln, Cl
+ Fl
(cresc.)
Vcl
+ Euph, Acc
Slightly faster
Lul-la-by
in the ci-ty
where dream sha-dows
Stgs, Ww,
Cymb (roll)
mf
sigh
+ Acc, Euph

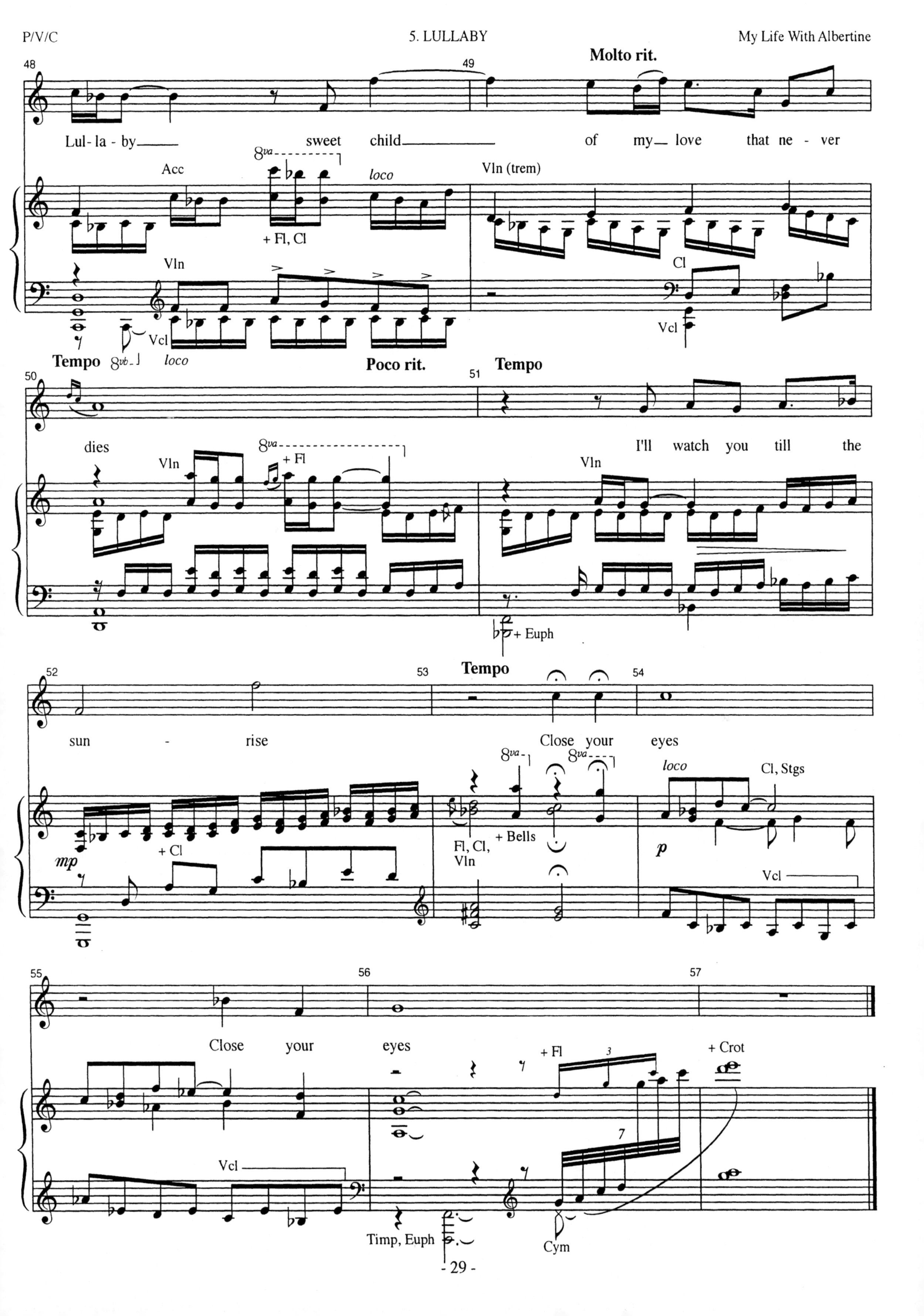
Molto rit.
Lul-la-by sweet child of my love that ne-ver
Acc
8va
loco
Vln (trem)
+ Fl, Cl
Vln
Cl
Vcl
Tempo
Poco rit.
Tempo
dies
I'll watch you till the
Vln
+ Fl
+ Euph
Tempo
sun - rise
Close your eyes
loco
Cl, Stgs
+ Cl
+ Bells
Fl, Cl, Vln
mp
p
Close your eyes
+ Fl
+ Crot
Timp, Euph
Cym

# FERRET SONG UNDERSCORE

Cue: "...I saw her, she was to appear different"

Segue as one

# O FERRET OF FAIRY WOOD

Cue: "Clearing on the cliff

11
12
13
+Bs Cl.
(Cl,Vln.)
cresc.
f
+Cl.
(Vcl.)
14
+Vln.
15
ALL THREE:
16
Oh Fer-ret of Fair - y Wood he just ran by.
Vln.
(Piano cued)
mf
+Tamb.
+Euph.
+Bs Cl.
17
18
19
Oh Fer-ret of Fair - y Wood he passed by me.
Oh Fer-ret of Fair - y Wood
20
ALBERTINE:
Whom will I mar - ry?
21
ALL:
Oh Fer-ret of Fair - y Wood
Poco rit.
22
ALBERTINE:
Whom will I love?

Tempo
24
ALL:
Molto rit.
Oh Fer-ret of Fair-y Wood now come to me.
(Cl. solo)
+Tamb.
cresc.
(Pno. play)
Tempo
Oh Fer-ret of Fair-y Wood take him my glove.
+Bells
8va
loco
Vln.
Cl.
+Acc.
(Cl. solo)
f
Tutti
mf
+Bs Cl,Euph.
Vcl.
+Tri.
+Low Tom
Sweet la-dies and gents did-dle and did-dle Sweet la-dies and gents did-dle di
+Acc.
(Vln. cued)
mp
(Cl. cued)
+Euph. (downbeat)
+Vcl. (pizz.)
ALBERTINE:
ALL:
do. Mar-ry I will Did-dle and did-dle
+Bs Cl.
+Vln.
+Bs Cl,Euph.
+Cl.
Vcl. (arco - sus.)

ALBERTINE:
GIRLS:
Rit.
Tempo
Just tell me who Did-dle di do.
Oh Fer-ret of Fair-y Wood where could he be?
+Acc
(Cl.)
(Pno. out)
+Bs Cl.
(Pno. play)
(Cl,Stgs.)
+Vcl.
+Euph.
Oh Fer-ret of Fair-y Wood where has he gone
ALBERTINE:
Poco rit.
ALL:
Molto rit.
ALBERTINE:
Oh Fer-ret of Fair-y Wood will I have child-ren? Oh Fer-ret of Fair-y Wood or will I have
+Xylo
mf
+Euph.
+Bs Cl,Vcl. (pizz.)
Tempo
none?
(Pno. out)
Cl.
Bs Cl.
Vcl.
Pno.
Pno.

ALL 3:
La la la la la la la la la la la
La la la la la la la la la la la
(Acc. cued)
+Cl.
+Bs Cl.
+Vcl. (pizz./gliss.)
+Vln.
+Acc.
+Cl,Vln.
+Cl,Vln.
Vcl. (arco)
They scream and stop dancing
and instinctively cover themselves
CUE: MARCEL: "can I play too?
+Vln.
59 A
(To 60)
+Sus Cym. roll
f
+Bs Cl.
+Cl.
+Vcl.
+TTs
(Cl. solo)
+Tamb.

60
ALBERTINE:
61
62
Oh Fer-ret of Fair-y Wood where could she be? Oh Fer-ret of Fair-y Wood where
ANDREE:
Oh Fer-ret of Fair - y Wood where could she be? Oh Fer-ret of
ROSAMUNDE:
Oh Fer-ret of Fair - y Wood where could he be?
MARCEL:
Oh Fer-ret of Fair - y Wood where could she
+Cl,Acc,Vln.)
+Euph.
+Bs Cl,Vcl. (pizz.)
63
64
has she gone? Oh Fer - ret of Fair - y Wood
Fair - y Wood where has she gone? Oh Fer - ret of
Oh Fer - ret of Fair - y Wood where has he gone?
be? Oh Fer - ret of Fair - y Wood where has she

65
66
Poco rit.
67
Rit.
will we have child - ren? oh Fer-ret of Fair-y Wood or
Fair-y Wood will we have child - ren? oh Fer-ret of Fair-y Wood or
Oh Fer-ret of Fair-y Wood will I have child - ren? Oh or
gone? Oh Fer-ret of Fair-y Wood will we have child - ren? oh
68
69
Tempo
70
71
72
will I have none?
will I have none?
will I have none?
will I have none?
loco
mp
+Sus Cym.
Euph.
Bs Cl.
Cl,Vcl. (pizz.)
(Pno. cued)
Tutti
Cl,Bs Cl,Euph
Acc,Pno,Vcl.
Attacca
+Cym choke

# O FERRET PLAYOFF

# UNDERSCORE AFTER "FERRET SONG"

# UNDERSCORE BEFORE "MY SOUL WEEPS"

Cue: "And we can play... at anything you choose."

Segue as one

# MY SOUL WEEPS

CUE: "Would you like me to read it to you?"

My soul weeps like rain and as it falls I hear it start to sing a sad and
+Fl,Acc.
Stgs.
+Vibes
+Bs Cl.
mourn-ful song that is emp-ty of ev'-ry-thing.
+Acc,Stgs.
+Sus Cym.
My soul weeps like rain up-on the ver-dant fields so far be-low I hate my
+Fl, Stgs. (Trem.)
mf
Bs Cl.
+Acc.
+Sus Cym.
f
+Bs Cl.
+Tbn.
heart It dis-gusts me Why do I hurt so?
mf
mp
+Stgs.
p
+Vibes
+Bs Cl.

Più mosso
Molto accel.
Molto rit.
+Acc. solo
+Tbn.
Tempo
mp
My soul weeps like rain A heav-y down-pour from the clouds a - bove
+Stgs.
+Vibes
+Sus Cym.
+Vibes,Tbn,Acc.
I weep with - out rea - son With - out an - y hate or
+Fl.
Fl.
f
+Bs Cl.
+Vibes
an - y love
+Acc,Vcl.
+Vla.
+Cym. scrape
+Fl,Acc.
+Bs Cl.
+Bs Cl.

MARCEL tries to join her
in her vocalise:
Bells interrupt
44
45
46
47
48
Ah
ah
ah
(Fl,Acc.)
8va
loco
Acc. solo
3
+Vla.
+Vcl.
+Tbn.
49
Alternate-if song ends!
50
8va
+Fl.
+Vibes

# SONATA FRAGMENT

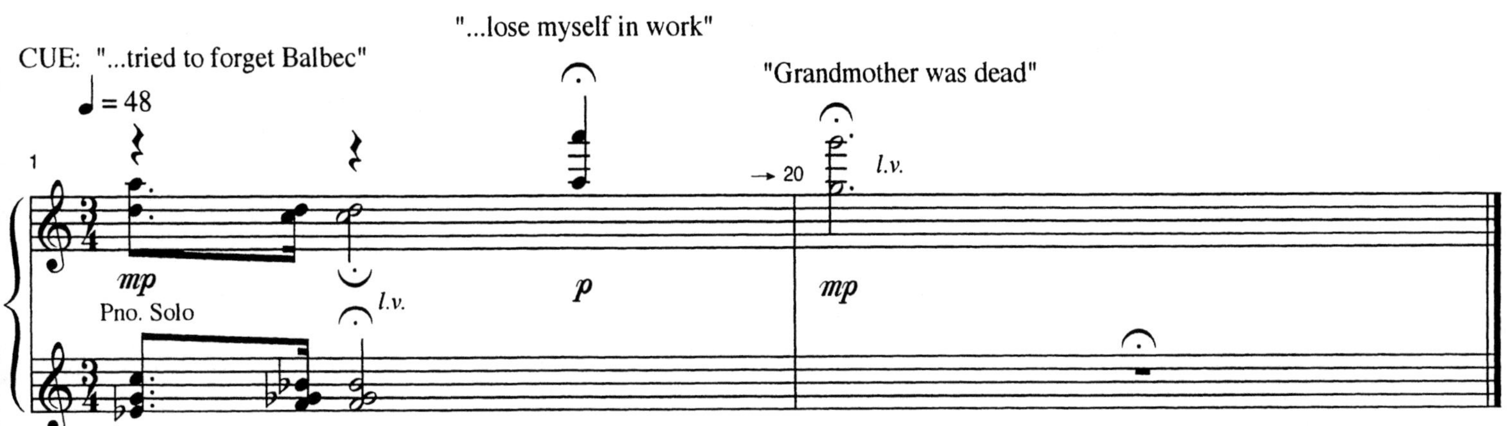


**Segue to "Prayer"**

This page left blank intentionally for page turns

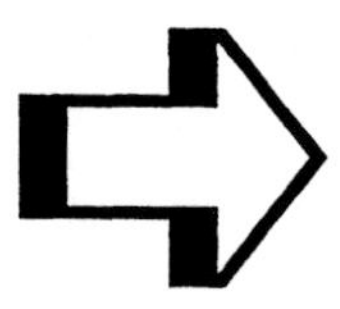

# THE PRAYER

CUE: "...wrote this instead"
Mournful (♩ = 66)
MARCEL & NARRATOR:
Oh God have pi - ty on my pain
+Fl,Cl. (only)
+Pno.
+Vcl,Timp.
+Vln.
+Crotales
Heal my hurt Let her live for - ev - er and
+Euph,Acc.
mf
(Vcl.)
ev - er Let us be to - ge - ther
+Acc.
(Pno. out)
+Cl,Stgs.
p
+Pno.
+Euph.

Take
pi - ty
Take
pi - ty
Oh
God
+Sus Cym.
+Euph,Acc.
+Fl. solo
+Cym. scrape
8va
(Cl,Stgs.)
mf
sfz
sfz
sfz
Chorus Hums:
Hmm...
Cl,Stgs.
loco
+Acc.
mp
+Vcl (pizz.),Timp.
mf

37
38
39
40
sfz
sfz
sfz
Fl,Vln.
+Cl,Vcl.
Sweeping
FRANCOISE:
41
42
43
Lul - la - bye in the ci - ty where dream sha - dows sigh
mf
+Euph,Sus Cym.
44
45
Lul - la - bye sweet child
+Fl,Cl.
8va
loco
+Acc.
+Euph,Vcl.
+Tam-tam
loco
8vb
Tempo
Rit.
Tempo
Poco rit.
46
47
of a love that ne - ver dies
Vln. (trem.)
+Fl.
8va
+Cl.
+Cym. Cr.

48
FRANCOISE:
She'll watch you till the sun - rise
49
Tempo I
50
CHORUS (SATB):
Oh God have pi - ty on my
+Vln.
+Fl.
+Cl,Vcl.
f
+Euph.
+Timp.
51
52
53
54
(CHORUS) pain
Heal my hurt
Let her live
for -
(Euph.)

55
56
57
58
p
ev - er and ev - er
Let us be to -
p
(Vln. solo)
mp
p
59
60
61
62
ge - ther
Take pi - ty Take
+Fl. solo
+Sus Cym.
mp
+Stgs.
f
63
64
65
pi - ty Take pi - ty Take pi - ty Take
8va
loco
8va
loco
+Cym. scrape
decresc.
8vb

**Segue to "Talk About the Weather"**

# TALK ABOUT THE WEATHER

9
10
11
12
Par - is? in Bal - bec? in Com - bray?
+Vln.
13
14
15
16
Talk a - bout which par - ty they could be at - tend - ing to -
17
18
19
FRANCOISE:
20
A change in the
day.
+Cym. roll
+Cl.
+Fl.
+Cym.

21
22
23
24
wea - ther
is all that it takes to be -
mf
+Euph.
25
26
27
Rit.
28
gin a - gain.
mp
sfz
+Vln. (Trem.)
mp
29
Tempo
30
31
32
MARCEL:
Talk a - bout this paint - er this
legato
+Stgs.

33
34
35
36
writ - er, the gos - sip, the hear - say.
37
38
39
40
Poco rit.
Talk of which draw - ing - room they could lan - guish long in to -
41
Tempo
42
43
FRANCOISE:
44
A change in the
day?
+Fl.
+Acc.
+Acc.
+Cl.
cresc.
+Cym. roll
+Cym. (brush)
+Tbn.

45
46
47
48
Rit.
wea - ther is all that it takes to be -
+Fl,Cl,Vln.
mf
+Tbn.
49
Tempo (più mosso)
50
51
52
gin a - gain.
I
I
+Vln. (Trem.)
Cl,Acc.
+Vln.
mp
cresc.
Vcl. (arco)
+Vcl. (pizz.)
+Sus Cym.
+Tbn.
53
54
55
56
think a - bout the wea - ther out - side the
think a - bout the wea - ther out - side the
+Fl,Cl
+Crotales
mf

57
58
59
Rit.
60
+Fl.
win - dow to - day, the fog that I watch slow - ly burn a -
win - dow to - day, the fog that I watch slow - ly burn a -
Vln.
Vln.
cresc.
+Cl.
61
(rit.)
62
63
Tempo
64
way. I think a - bout the
way. I think a - bout the
f
mp
65
66
67
Rit.
68
light in - side the room to - day, think a - bout light fal - ling
light in - side the room to - day, think a - bout light fal - ling
Stgs.(Trem.),Fl.
+Cl.
+Vcl.

Slower
Molto rit.
fine rain across that
fine rain across that
Pno. solo
+Sus Cym.
♩= 66
Rit.
let-ter tray. I think I'll stay
let-ter tray. I think I'll stay
+Fl,Vln.
loco
+Cl.
+Acc.
cresc.
+Vcl.
+Tbn.
+Sus Cym.
Tempo
Rit.
home again to-day.
home again to-day.
Tutti
+Vibes
decresc.

Tempo I
FRANCOISE: (humming)
INSTRUMENTAL
+Vln,Acc. (cued in Fl.)
+Vcl. (pizz.)
Rit.
Tempo
(Instr.)
+Cl.
Vcl. (arco)
MARCEL: (humming)
+Acc.
+Fl,Vln.
+Cym. (brush)
+Sus Cym.

Broadening
ALL: including FRANCOISE + MARCEL
WOMEN:
A change in the wea - ther is
MEN:
A change in the wea - ther is
mf
+Cl.
Rit.
all that it takes or so they
all that it takes or so they
+Fl.
+Bells
Meno mosso
say.
say.
Fl,Vln.
+Acc.
Vcl.
+Cl.
+Tbn.
+Sus Cym.
+Vcl.
+Bells
mf
V.S. to PLAYOFF

CUE: "and then the sun came out"

# THE DIFFERENT ALBERTINES

play solo softly as underscore, *Molto rubato,* follow dialogue cues. Band in at m.40.

Cue: "If you're busy, you needn't see me.Goodnight"

Rit.
Tempo
("near my home")
8vb
("where is she?")
Accel.
8vb

Slower
Accel.
("annoyed")
Slower
("silence then...")
Accel.
Rit.
8vb
Rit.
("Come right over")
("pause")
[agitato w/arguing]
Rit.
("nuisance")
f
mp

Cue Band
Accel.
Rit.
("calm down")
Rubato, back to ♩ = 116
+Cls,Vln.
mp
+Vcl.
+Sus Cym.
Cue:(Narrator sings to the audience, leaning now on the piano, as the pianist behind plays.)
Rit.
NARRATOR:
Al - ber - tine...
+Cls,Acc,Vln.
(Vcl.)
Tempo
Rit.
Al - ber - tine...
+Cls,Acc,Vln.
Tempo
Rit.
A sil - hou - ette a - gainst the sea, and
(Vcl.)

50
Tempo
ev - 'ry - time I look I
cresc.
+Vln.
51
Rit.
see a diff - 'rent
52
Tempo
Al - ber - tine,
mf
53
54
Al - ber -
55
Rit.
tine
56
Meno mosso, stricter
Cls.
grazioso
mp
Vcl.
57
A
+Tbn.
58
girl in Bal - bec with
+Vln.
Vcl.
+Tri.
59
plump cheeks she
+Tbn.
60
bold - ly stares from those

61
62
63
stairs where the street and beach meet.
8va
A
64
Rubato ♩ = 116
65
66
67
Rit.
sil - hou - ette a - gainst the sea, and ev - 'ry - time I look I see a diff - 'rent
+Acc.
+Vln.
+Cls.
+Cls, Vln.
cresc.
+Vcl.
+Vcl.
+Sus Cym.
68
Tempo
69
70
Al - ber - tine, Al - ber -
f
+Tbn.
+Vcl.
Vcl w/Acc.
71
Rit.
Meno mosso,
72
stricter ♩ = 80
73
tine
A
+Cls, Vln.
mp
+Bells
+Tbn, Vcl.

74
75
76
girl with red hair and beau - ty spot u - pon chin and a
+Bells
77
78
thin ring - ing laugh like coo - ing doves
sfz
mf
+Tbn.
79
Molto rit.
80
Tempo ♩ = 116
81
— mak - ing love.
A
8va
+Vln.
+Cl. 2
+Cl. 1
f
+Vcl.
82
Tempo
83
84
85
Rit.
sil - hou - ette a - gainst the sea, and ev - 'ry - time I look I see a diff - 'rent
+Vln. (Trem.)
+Cls.
+Acc.
+Cls, Vln.
p
cresc.
+Vcl.

Tempo
Al - ber - tine,
+Cls,Vln,Bells
+Tbn.
mf +Vcl.
+Sus Cym.
Poco meno mosso (stricter)
Rit.
Her hands strain out a leash for hounds or la - zi - ly pau - sing lost in
+Cls.
+Bells
mp +Stgs.
cresc. +Vcl. (pizz.)
+Tbn.
Tempo
Molto rall.
Tempo, expansive
dreams, or sud den - ly stretch - ing out
Oh
+Cls.
+Vln. (Trem.)
+Acc.
Al - ber - tine.
Oh
Al - ber - tine.
Oh
+Cls,Vln.
ff +Vcl.
+Tbn,Acc.

Rit.
Tempo, meno mosso
MARCEL & NARRATOR:
Al - ber - tine.
A
+Cls.
+Vcl.
+Vln. (pizz.)
+Acc. (cued in Vln.)
+Tbn.
sil - hou - ette a - gainst the sea,
and ev - 'ry - time I look I
(cued in Vln.)
+Vln. (play), Cls
cresc.
+Tbn.
+Vcl.
Rubato ♩ = 116
see a diff - 'rent...
Vcl. (Trem.)
+Acc.
Tutti
+Vln.

116
Rit.
117
♩= 80
MARCEL:
118
Oh
+Cls,Vln.
sub. mp
119
Al - ber - tine.
p
120
Slower
mp
121
Slower
NARRATOR:
122
123
Rit.
124
125
126
Each time I look I see a diff - 'rent
+Cl,Acc. (cued in Vln.)
+Vln.
+Vcl
+Bs Cl.
+Timp. roll
127
♩= 116
128
129
130
(to 135)
you.
+Bells,Vln.
+Vcl.
+Sus Cym.
+Cl.

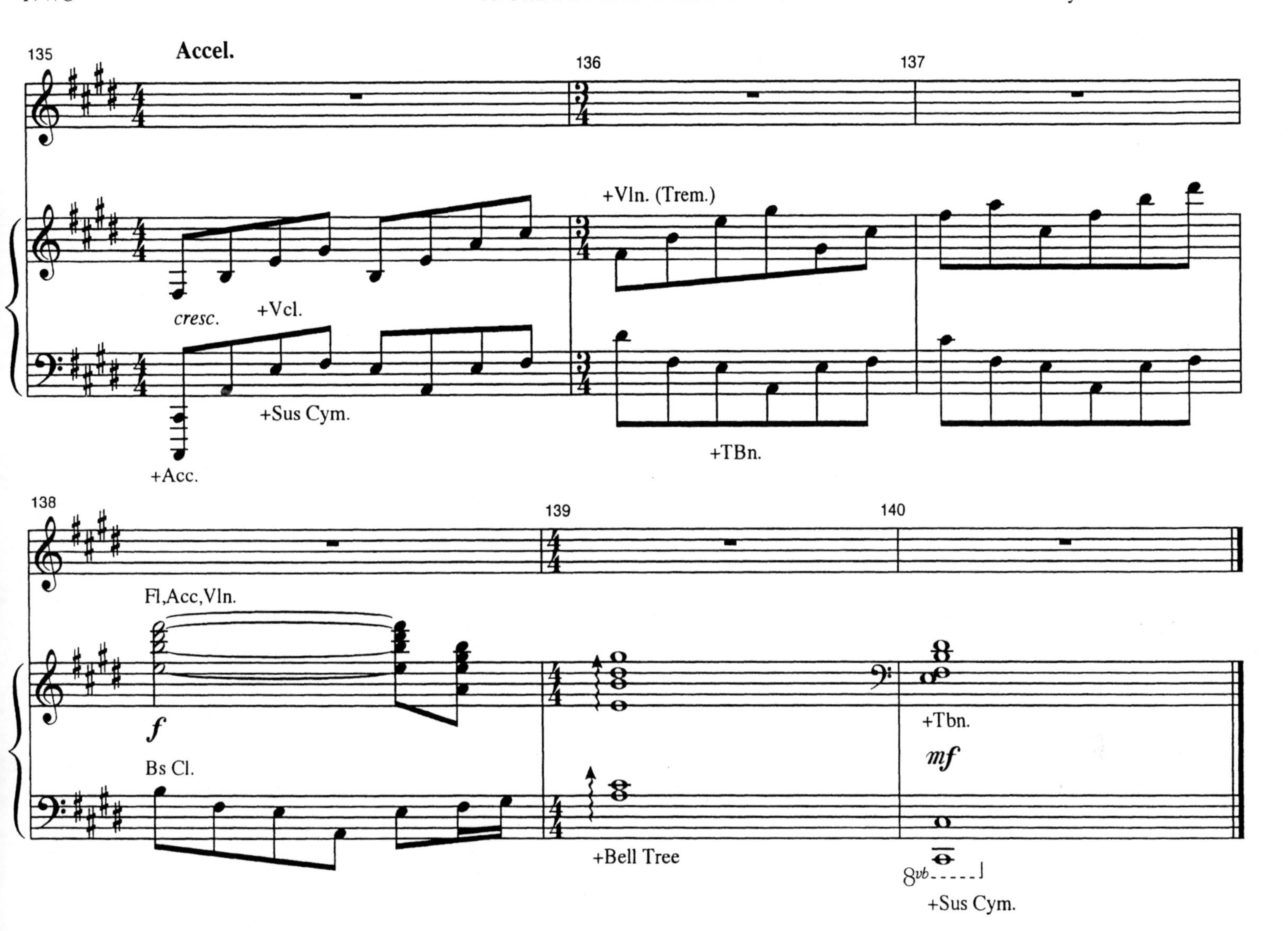
135
Accel.
136
137
+Vln. (Trem.)
cresc.
+Vcl.
+Sus Cym.
+TBn.
+Acc.
138
139
140
Fl,Acc,Vln.
f
Bs Cl.
+Tbn.
mf
+Bell Tree
8vb
+Sus Cym.

# SAD BALBEC

18
+Bs Cl.
19
20
21
22
+Vln.
(Vcl.)
23
24
25
26
27
+Acc. (cued in Vln.)
mp
28
29
30
+Vln.
31
32
33
+Acc.
34
35
+Cl.
+Vcl.
36
+Tri.
37
38
39
+Acc.
40
41
42
43

**Più mosso**
**Safety (Jump on cue to m. 53)**
"...drink at the little casino near the station."

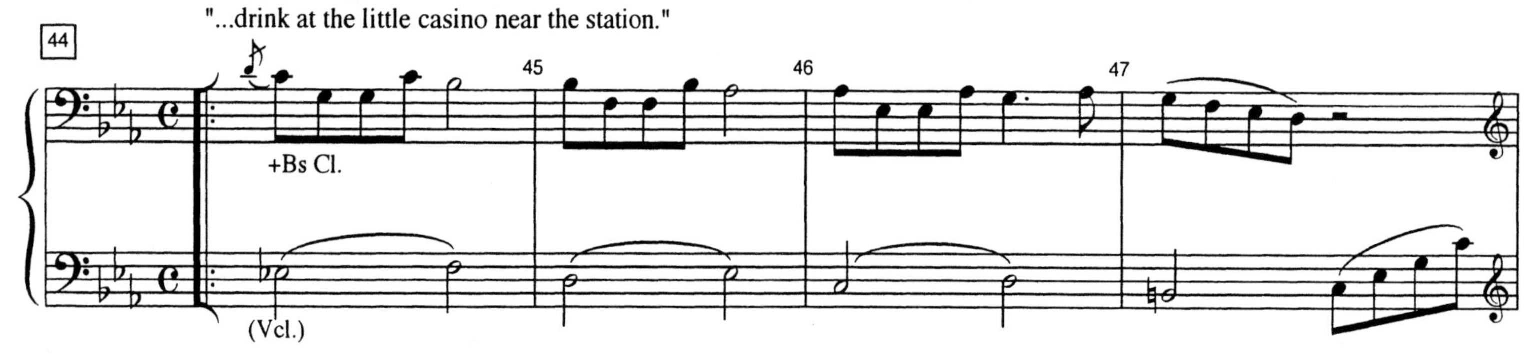


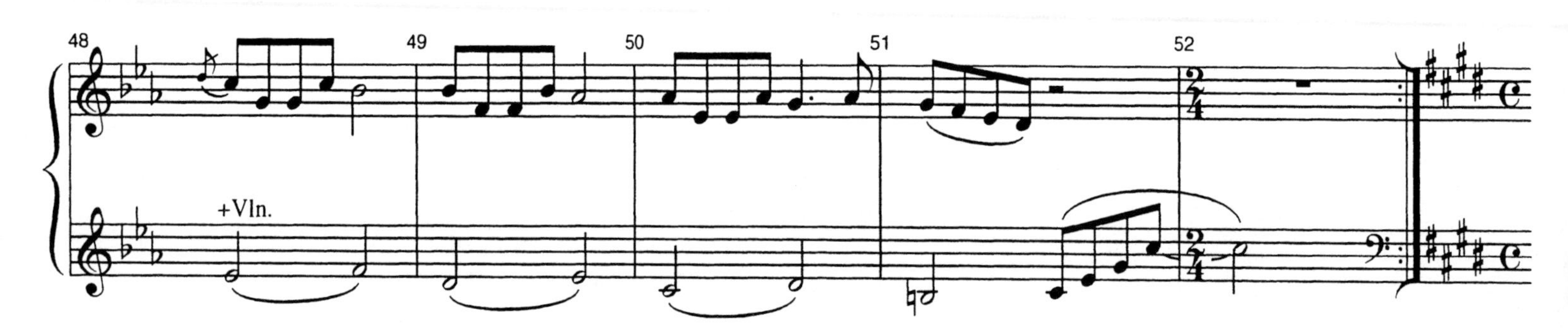


**Safety (Jump on cue to #9 "My Soul Weeps/Tango")**
"...dancing together."

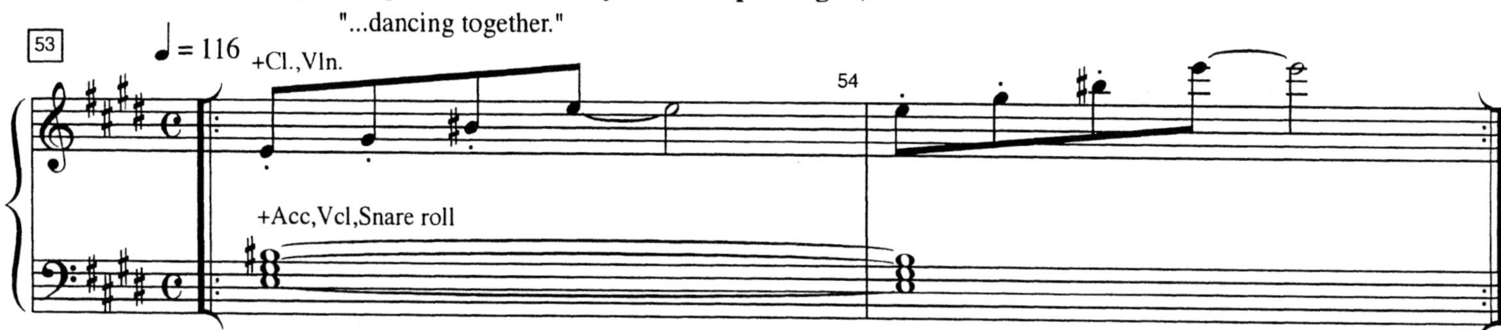


**Segue as one**

# MY SOUL WEEPS/TANGO

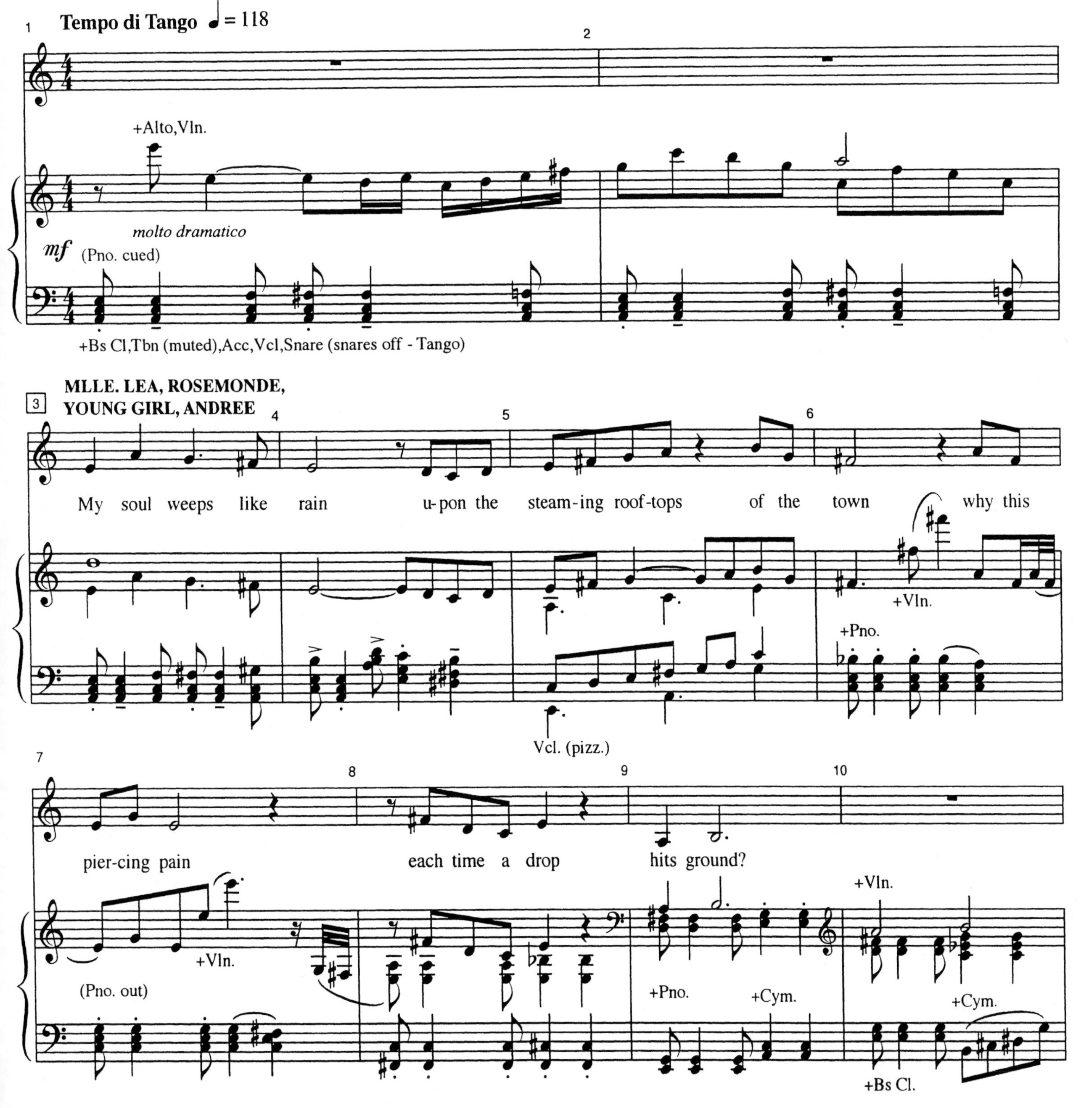

My soul weeps like rain and as it falls I hear it start to sing a sad and
mourn-ful song that is emp - ty of ev'-ry-thing
+Alto
+Acc.
+Euph.
+Vln.
+Acc,Vln.
Pno. solo
Safety
Vamp
CUE TO CONTINUE: "I can't see their faces"
CUE TO CONTINUE: "nipples"
Alto,Vln. (1st x only)
Acc,Vcl.
Tbn,Vcl. (1st x only)
+Snare (1st x only)
+Vln.
+Tbn.
Safety
CUE TO CONTINUE: "breasts"
(To 28)
Alto,Vln.
+Tenor
+Sn.
+Castanets
+Tbn,Vcl.

ROSEMONDE:
28
(preferred vocal)
29
30
31
My soul weeps like rain u-pon the ver-dant fields so far be - low I hate my
(alternate simpler vocal)
My soul weeps like rain u-pon the ver-dant fields so far be - low I hate my
Vln.
Sxs.
Tbn.
+Acc.
Vln.
32
33
34
35
heart it dis - gusts me. Why do I hurt so?
heart it dis - gusts me Why do I hurt so?
36
(vocalise)
37
38
Molto rit.
39
Ah Ah
+Alto
+Acc.
+Vln.

40
Tempo
41
42
43
My soul weeps like rain a heavy down-pour from the clouds a - bove.
My soul weeps like rain a heavy down-pour from the clouds a - bove.
+Acc. gliss.
+Cym.
+Vln.
44
45
46
I weep with - out rea - son, with - out a - ny
I weep with - out rea - son with - out a - ny
Sxs,Stgs.
+Vln.
Tbn.
47
48
49
hate, or a - - - ny
hate, or a - - - ny
+Sn.
Pno. solo
+Bell of Cym.
+Vcl.

50
51
52
53
Safety
53A
(To 54)
love.
ABRUPT STOP ON:
"Albertine!"
love.
+Acc.
(long)
+Snare
54
CUE: At the hotel's
dining room
+Vln.
55
56
57
58
(Instrumental Underscore)
+Vcl.
59
(Vln.)
60
61
62
(Vcl.)
63
64
65
66

67
68
69
70
71
72
73
74
75
+Stgs. (trem. harm.)
76
(To 79)
Pno. solo
Safety
CUE TO CONTINUE: "...behind me, a huge mirror"
79
+Vln.
80
+Cl.
+Vcl.
81
2x
Cl,Vln.
82
83
84
Vcl.

85
86
87
Cl.
Vcl.
88
CUE TO CONTINUE: "I can't see their faces"
Poco rit.
89
+Vln.
90
91
92
Vcl.
93
Tempo
+Vln.
94
95
96
97
98
99
100
101
+Cl.
102
102A
102B
(To 103)

103
104
JUMP ON CUE: "I'll go tomorrow"
Safety
105
106
Vln.
+Vcl.
107
Acc,Vln.
Vcl.
108+Cl,Tbn.
109
Vln.
p
109A
109B
109C
109D
+Vcl.
p
109E
109F
109G
109H
109I
109J
109K

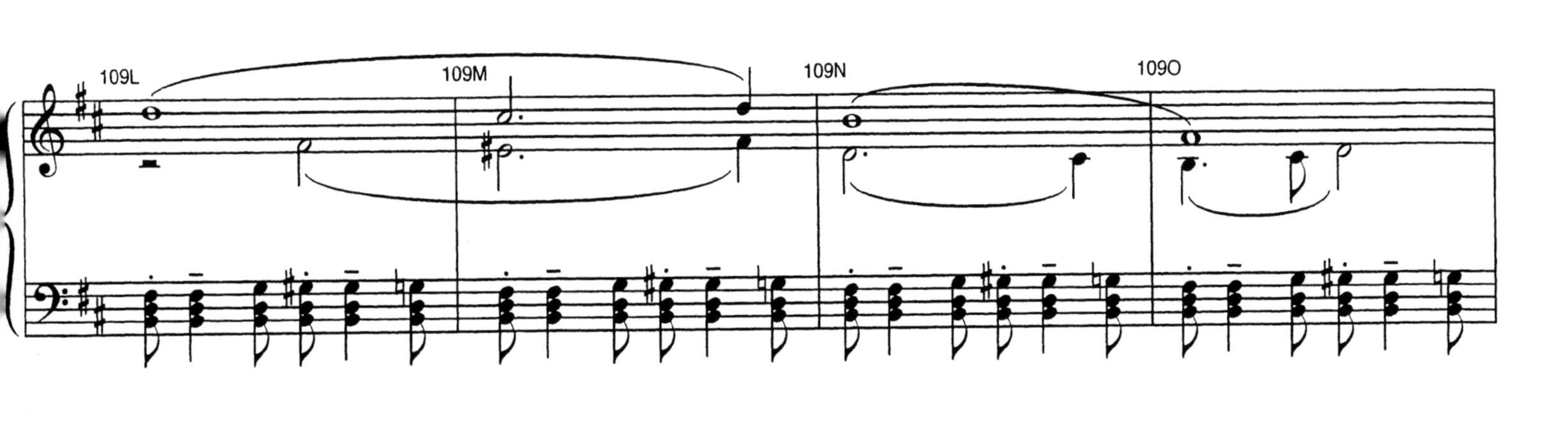
109L
109M
109N
109O

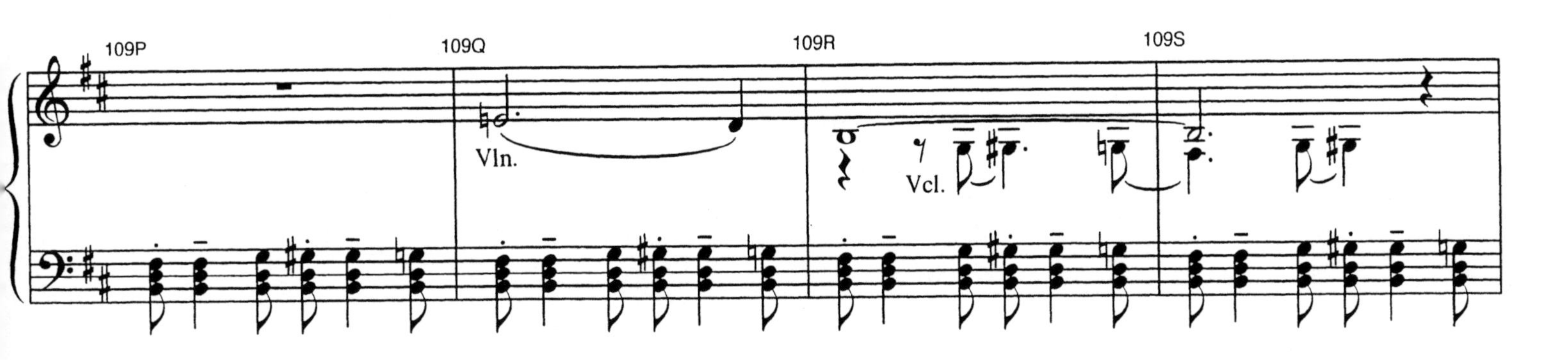
109P
109Q
Vln.
109R
Vcl.
109S

109T
109U
109V
Safety
(To 110)

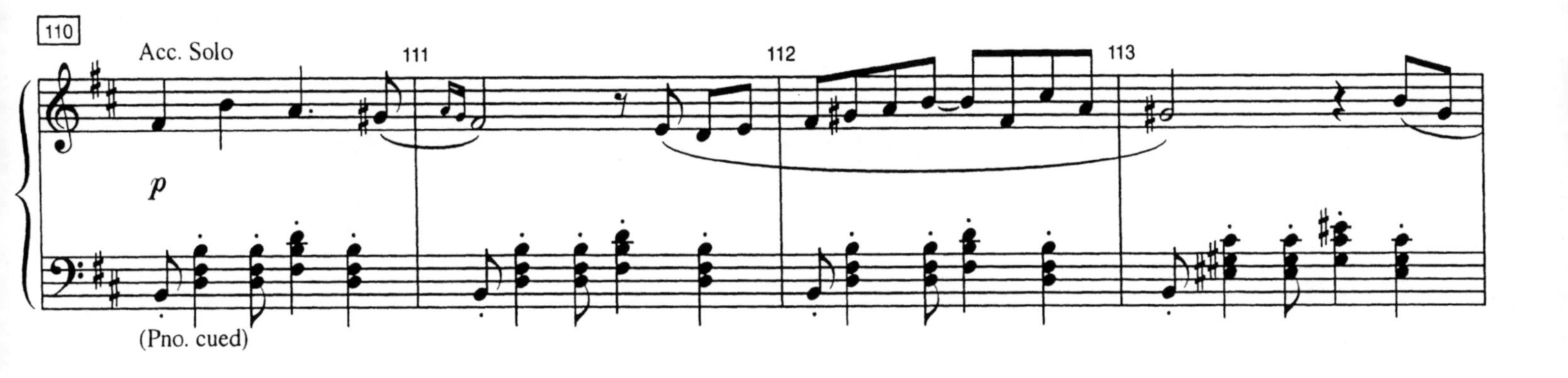
110
Acc. Solo
p
(Pno. cued)
111
112
113

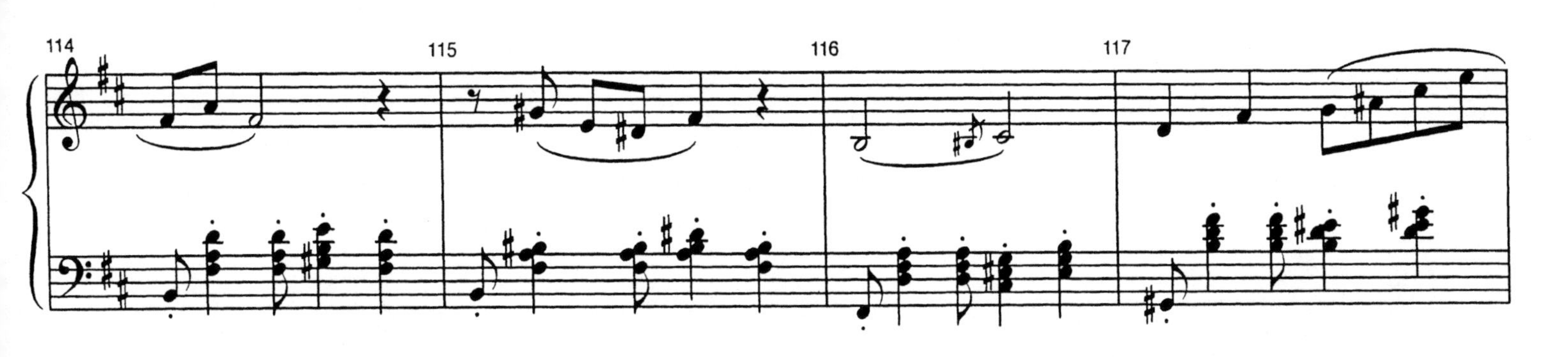
114
115
116
117

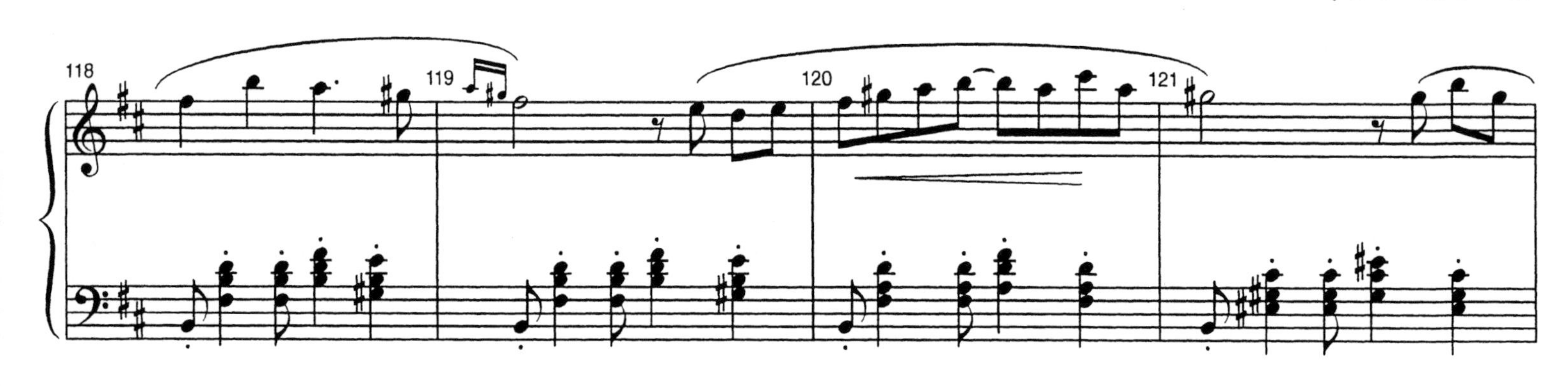
118
119
120
121

122
123
124
3
125

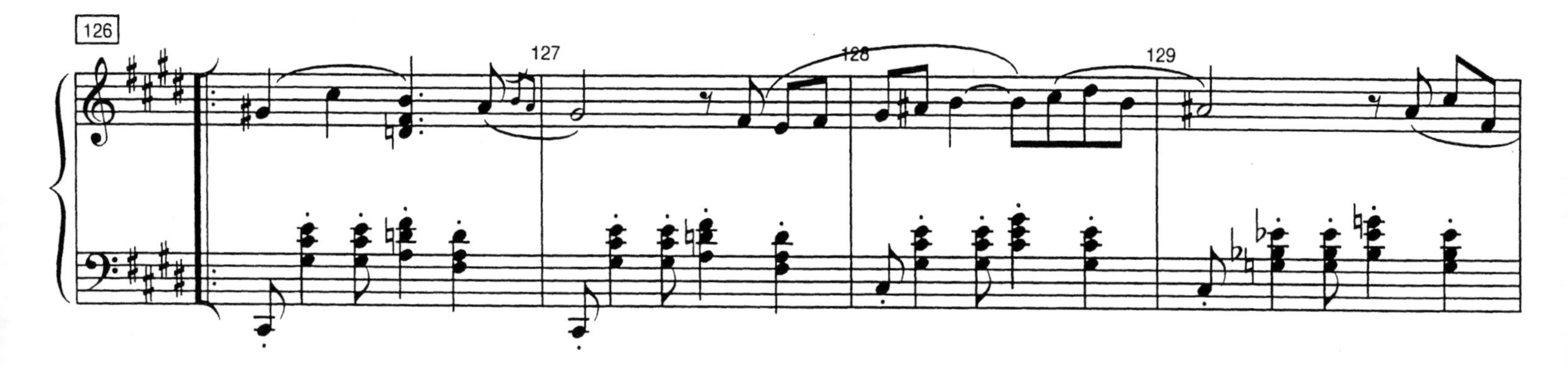
126
127
128
129

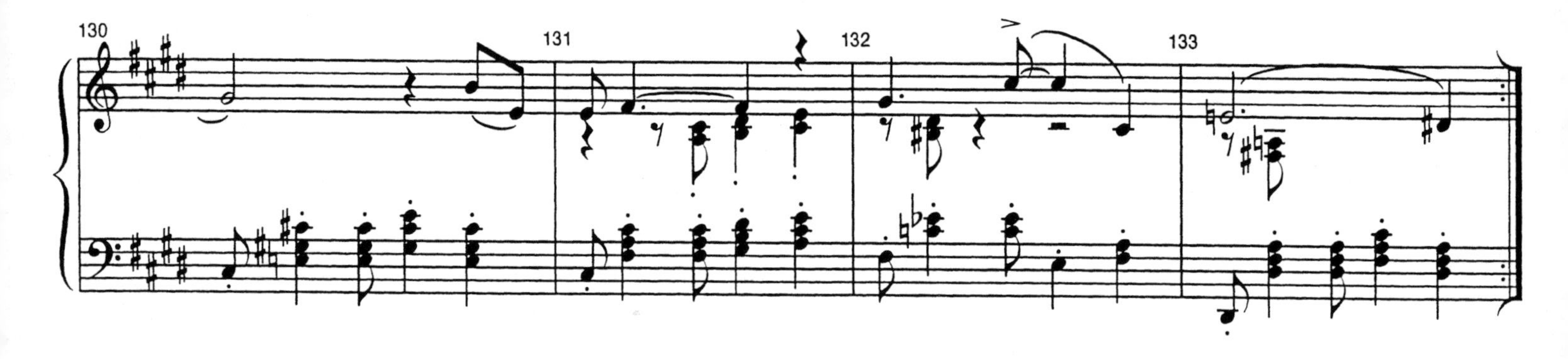
130
131
132
133

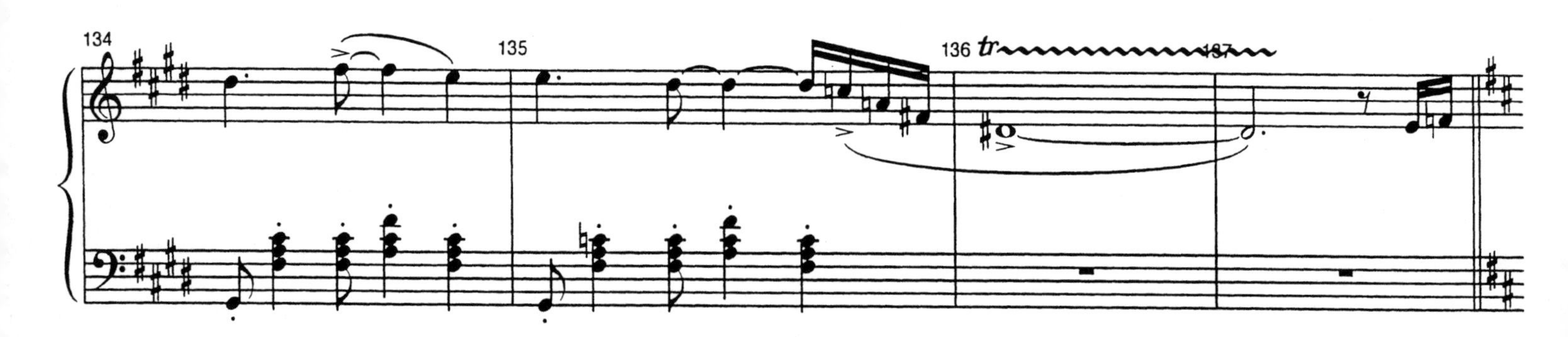
134
135
136
tr
137

138
139
140
141
(Acc.)
(Pno. play)
142
143
144
145
Safety
Safety
Vamp
CONTINUE ON CUE: "thank you for explaining to me"
146
147
148
+Alto,Sop. Sx.
+Stgs.
+Tbn,Vcl,Acc.
+Snare
149
150
151
My soul weeps like
My soul weeps like
+Sop.
+Vln.
+Vln.
+Alto
Sxs,Vln.
Tbn,Acc,Vcl,Snare
+Snare roll
+Cr.

152
153
154
rain a hea - vy down - pour from the clouds a - bove
rain a hea - vy down - pour from the clouds a - bove
(Sop.)
Tutti
155
156
157
158
I weep with - out rea - son with - out a - ny hate, or
I weep with - out rea - son with - out a - ny hate, or
+Castanets
Tbn,Acc,Vln.
159
160
161
162
a - ny - love.
a - ny - love.
Sop. solo
+Tam-tam roll
Tutti
Alto
Sxs,Tbn.
Stgs,Acc,Tbn. (sus)

# BUT WHAT I SAY IS...

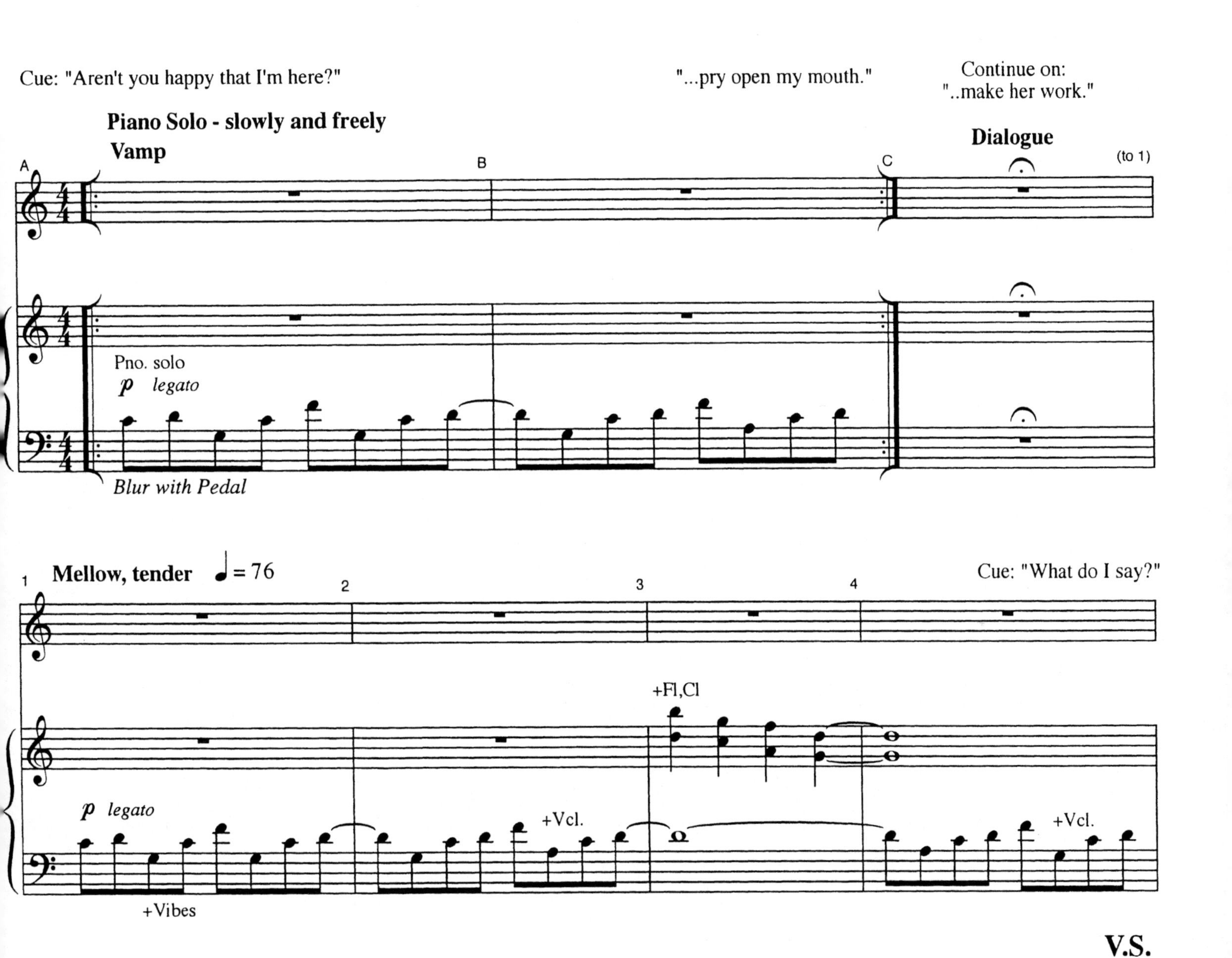


V.S.

NARRATOR:
Love me, is what you think but what you say is
MARCEL:
Kiss me Hold me
+Acc. (cued in Fl.)
+Stgs.
+Tri.
+Tbn.
+ALBERTINE:
Kiss me Hold me
NARRATOR:
but what you think is
+Fl,Cl.
+Acc.
+Cym.
+Stgs. (Trem. + harm.)
+Tbn,Stgs. (ord.)
+Vibes
Want me is all you think
MARCEL:
but what I say is:
Touch me. Please me.
+ALBERTINE:
Touch me. Please me.
+Acc. (cued in Fl.)
+Stgs.
+Fl,Cl,Stgs. (Trem + harm.)
+Tri.
+Tbn.
NARRATOR:
but what you think is
18 Più mosso
Like me. Love me.
MARCEL:
Need me. But what I say is:
+Acc.
+Fl,Cl.
+Sus Cym.
loco
Fl.
+Crotales
+Vln.
+Vcl.
+Tbn,Stgs. (ord.)
mf
Cl.

ALBERTINE:
Rit.
Tempo
Have– me. Have—— me
MARCEL:
Have me Have me
NARRATOR: But what you think is
Don't hurt me.
+Fl,Cl.
+Acc.
(Stgs.)
+Tbn.
mp
mf
+Vcl,Tbn.
Rit.
NARRATOR:
MARCEL:
Don't leave me. Don't lie to me.—— But what I say is
+Vln.
+Fl.
+Acc.
+Cl.
mf
+Vcl.
sub. mp
+Tbn,Vln.
+Acc,Vln. +Cl.
p
(Vcl.)
+Sus Cym.
Tempo (♩ = 88)
ALBERTINE:
Kiss me Kiss– me Kiss—
W/NARRATOR:
MARCEL:
NARR.
Kiss me Kiss— me Tongue— me But what I think is Love me Love– me Love—
+Bells
+Tbn.

me
Kiss me Kiss me tongue me
me
Kiss me Kiss me tongue me
+Fl.
Love me Love me Love me
Rit.
NARRATOR:
But all I say is
8va
+Sus Cym.
f
Tempo
ALBERTINE:
Tick-le me
Molto rit.
NARRATOR:
So all I say is
Tempo
ALBERTINE:
Tick - le me Tick-le me Tick-le
MARCEL:
Tick-le me Tick-le me So all I say is Tick - le me Tick-le me Tick-le
+Cl,Acc,Vln.
Fl.
ff
sub. f +Cym. scrape
+Tri. roll
+Tbn,Vcl.

Rit.
Tempo
Accel.
41
42
Tick - le me
Tick - le Tick-le me
Stgs. (Trem.)
+Fl.
+Acc.
Vln.
Cl.
+Vcl.
+Tri. roll
+Tbn.
43
44 They both laugh.
45
+Fl.
+Tbn,Vcl.
Applause segue

This page left blank intentionally for page turns

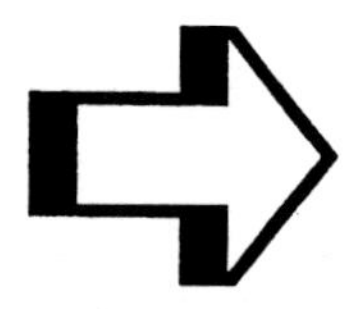

# SONG OF SOLITUDE

(no #12)

Rit.
meant or what's be - hind what's be - hind On
+Vln.
8va
mp +Sxs,Tbn.
+Vcl. (pizz.)
Slow, Plangent ♩ = 60
+Acc. solo,Stgs.
Poco rit.
a - ny giv - en day half the hu - man race is in tears, is in tears On
mp
+Tbn.
Tempo
Rit.
a - ny giv - en day half the hu - man race is in tears, is in
mf
mp
Acc,Vcl.
+Vcl.
Abrupt, Ironic ♩ = 84
tears
+Sxs,Tbn.
Sop. + Vln.
Sxs,Tbn.
sub. mf
+Acc.

Poco rit.
Tempo
Some say ly - ing is es - sen - tial to man-
+Vln. solo
+Acc.
Acc. (cued in Cl.)
+Tri.
sim.
7
+Vcl. (pizz.)
+Tbn.
kind, to man - kind Just a part of what the
+Vln. solo
+Xylo
+Cl.
Acc. (cued in Cl.)
+Alto,Tbn.
+Tri.
+Tbn.
+Vcl. (pizz.)
Rit.
good Lord had in mind had de - signed On
+Alto,Acc. (cued in Cl.)
+Mark Tree
legato
decresc.

♩= 60
+Stg,Acc. solo
a - ny giv - en day half the hu - man race is in tears, is in
+Tenor (cued in Alto)
mp
Poco rit.
Tempo
tears On a - ny giv - en day half the hu - man race is in
mf
mp +Alto
+Sus Cym.
+Tbn.
Poco accel.
Rall.
tears, is in tears I'm
Vln.
Acc,Vcl.
+Sxs,Acc,Stgs.
cresc.
+Sus Cym.
+Tbn.
Più mosso
♩= 69
told each one of us is all a - lone We long for, we pray for, we
tr
+Alto
mf
+Tbn,Vcl.

43
44
45
Rit.
search, we roam Like dogs we wait for some e - lu - sive bone. There's
+Bells
46
Slower
47
Colla voce
48
no such thing as heart, as hope, as home. On
+Vln. (muted)
Sxs,Tbn.
+Acc.
Acc. solo
sub. mp
p
+Vcl. (muted)
+Vcl.
49
Slower, quieter = 52
50
51
a - ny giv - en day half the hu - man race is in tears, is in
+Bells
p
+Vcl.

Rit.
52
53
54
tears
On
a - ny giv - en day half the
hu - man race is in
8va
loco
+Acc.
cresc.
+Sus Cym.
mf
mp
+Vcl.
(rit)
Slowly, oozing
55
56
57
58
tears,
is
in
tears
Stgs. (Trem. + harm.)
+Tenor
+Sus Cym.
+Vln.
p
Pno. solo
Acc,Stgs.
mf
+Tri.

End of Act 1

# I WANT YOU

Cue: "music"

15 **In 1** 𝅗𝅥. = 53 (♩ = 159) 16 17 18

+Snare (brushes)

*mp*

+Acc,Vcl.

19 **Brisk**
**MLLE. LEAH:** 20 21 22 23

I have seen in your heart the fires of your

+Vcl.

+Tbn.

Pno. solo *mf* *f*

8va

35
36
37
38
love
And I long to
+Vln.
+Sus Cym.
Bs Cl,Vcl.
f +Cl,Tbn,Acc.
mp
+Vcl. solo
39
40
41
42
throw a - way for - ev - er and a
+Sn. (brushes)
mf
+Cls,Tbn,Acc,Vln
43
44
45
46
day These tears and this
+Vln.
47
48
49
50
sad - ness too, and this
+Cl,Acc,Vln.
+Bs Cl,Vcl.

mad - ness too! Oh I
+Stgs. (trem.)
+Acc.
+Cl,Tbn.
mp
+Bs Cl.
+Sus Cym.
f
+Tbn,Cym.
want you Oh I
Cl.
8va
+Acc.
mp
+Bs Cl,Tbn,Stgs.
+Snare roll
want you
Rit.
loco +Cym.
+Vln.
3
+Cl.
mp
+Bs Cl.
63
Tempo
I have seen in your eyes the heat of your
+Acc.
mf
+Cl,Bs Cl.
+Tbn. (harmon)

68
69
70
71
72
+Acc.
love, my love
I have
+Vln.
+Acc,Vln.
+Vcl. (trem.)
+Cls.
+Cls,Tbn,Vcl.
+Vcl.
73
74
75
Rall.
76
felt in my thighs the raw meat of your
+Cl,Acc,Vln.
+Sus Cym.
77
Tempo
78
79
80
81
82
love, my love
And I long to
+Cl,Tbn,Acc,Stgs. (trem.)
+Bs Cl,Vcl. (pizz.)
+Cym
+Bs Cl.

83
84
85
86
throw a - way for - ev - er and a
mp
+Cl,Tbn.Stgs.
87
88
89
90
+Cl,Acc.
day These tears and this
+Sus Cym. (brushes)
+Bs Cl.
91
92
93
94
sad - ness too, and this
+Vln.
Acc.
+Cl.
+Sus Cym.
+Bs Cl.
+Tbn.
+Bs Cl.
95
96
97
98
Rall.
mad - ness too! Oh I
Vln,Cl.
f
+Sus Cym.
+Timp,Vcl.
+Bs Cl,Tbn.

99
Tempo
100
101
102
want
you
Oh
I
+Vln.
Cl,Acc.
Acc.
mf
103
104
105
Rit.
106
want
you
Cl,Tbn.
+Mark Tree (gliss.)
Bs Cl,Acc,Stgs. (sus)
cresc.
107
Tempo, Intense, poco più lento
108
109
110
I
have
no
re
-
grets
my
love
Cl.
f
+Tbn.
111
112
113
Rit.
114
on
-
ly
one
wish
to
make
to
live
+Vln.
+Cym
+Cls,Acc.
+Vcl.

115
Tempo
116
117
118
side by side,
heart to heart,
+Vln. (trem.)
8va
mp
+Cl,Vcl. (pizz.)
sfz
cresc. poco a poco
+Snare
+Acc.
+Bs Cl.
119
120
121
122
lip to lip,
ne - ver to part as your
loco
+Cl.
+Bs Cl.
123
Accel.
124
125
126
bo - dy's mine
My flesh thine,
+Sn. roll
Vcl. (arco)
127
128
129
130
I am the bread and you are the wine and I
Cls,Stgs,Acc. (sim.)
Vcl,Bs Cl.

131
132
133
134
Rit.
drink you,
drink you,
drink you, I
loco
Acc.
sfz
6
+Tbn.
+Cr.
Bs Cl.
+Snare roll
135
Broader
136
+Alto
137
138
Molto rit.
drink
you
8va
loco
sfz
ff
Vcl.
3
+Sus Cym.
Bs Cl,Tbn.
139
Tempo
+Vln.
140
141
142
Rit.
143
I have felt on your lips
the
Alto
+Sop Sx.
f
Acc.
8vb

144
Tempo
145
146
147
148
lust
of your love. I have
Vln.
+Alto
+Alto
mf
+Sop,Vcl.
+Vcl.
+Snare (brushes)
+Low Tom
+Low Tom
149
150
151
Rit.
152
heard from your lips the dis - trust of your
Acc,Stgs.
+Sxs.
Tbn.
+Cym
153
Tempo
154
155
156
Rit.
157
158
Slow
love, my love. And I long to
+Acc,Stgs.
+Sxs.
+Vln. (trem.)
+Vln.
Sop,Vln.
f
+Cym.
ff
Stgs. (trem.)
+Cr.
+Bell of Cym.
+Tbn.
Alto,Vcl.
+Vcl.

Tempo I
throw a - way for - ev - er and a
+Vln.
Rit.
Pno. solo
mp +Cym
+Sop,Vcl.
Vcl,Tbn.
Tempo
Rit.
Tempo
day these tears and this sad - ness
mf
+Cym.
f
+Vln. (trem.)
+Sus Cym.
Rit.
Rit.
Allargando
(opt.)
gliss.
too, and this mad - ness too! Oh I
Sxs,Tbn,Vln,Acc.
Sxs,Acc,Vln
Vln. (trem.)
ff
+Timp.
+Vcl (trem.),Acc,Timp.
Presto
want you.
Sxs.
+Vln.
f Vcl,Acc.
Tutti
8va
+Timp.
Applause segue

# I WANT YOU (PLAYOFF)

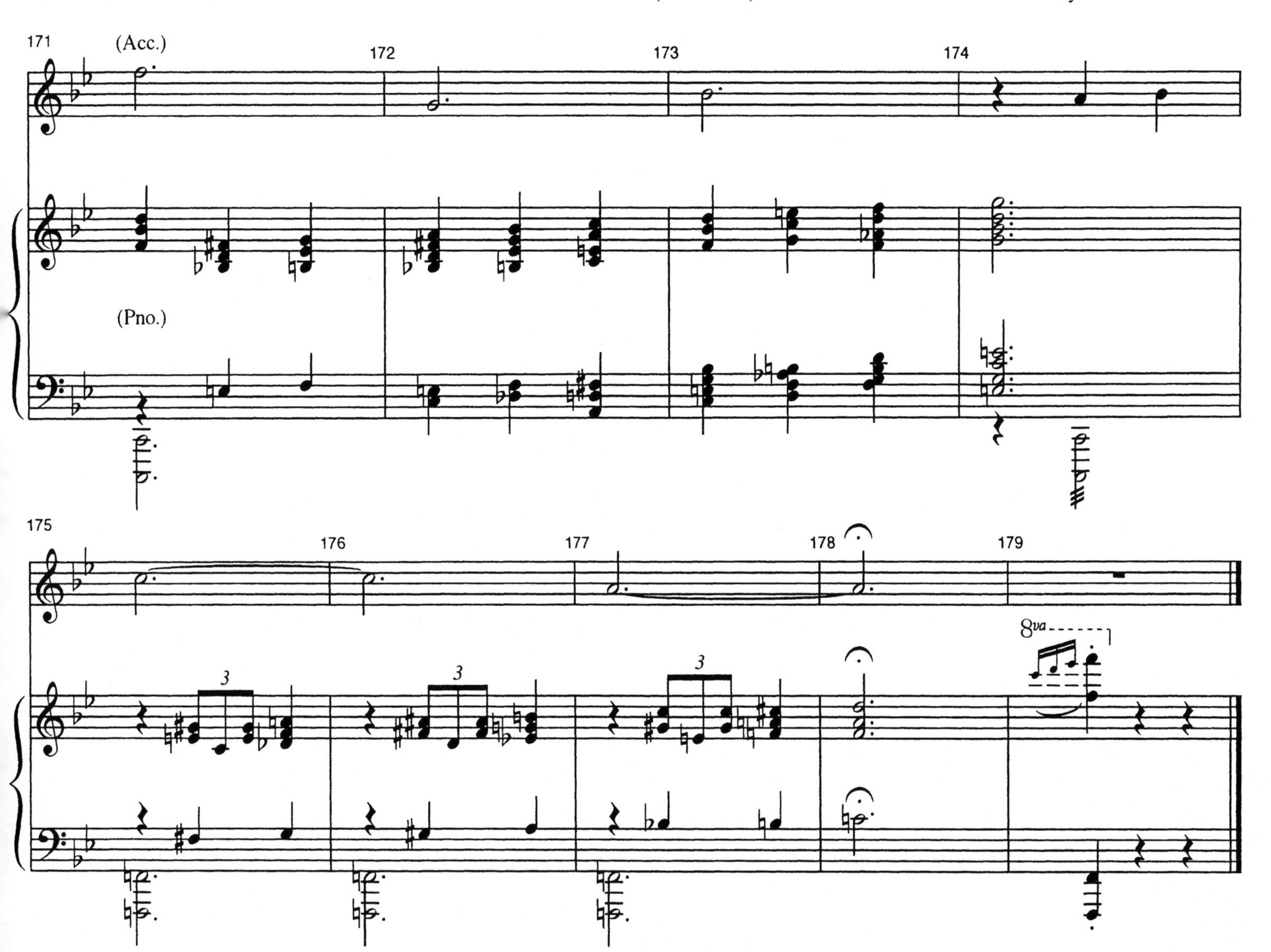
171
(Acc.)
172
173
174
(Pno.)
3
175
176
177
178
179
8va

# I NEED ME A GIRL

11
12
13
Rit.
14
lost his good job, and gone off and got sick. Now he
+Cls,Tbn.
+Acc.
15
Slower
16
17
Rit.
18
comes to my door, and he knocks there three times, and
+Tbn.
+Vcl.
19
Slow
20
21
22
this is what I hear him whine: I
+Vln.
+Acc.
+Cym.
loco
+Vcl. (pizz.)
V.S.

♩= 138 accel. poco a poco
need me a girl Oh give me a girl, I
+Vln.
+Tbn. (quasi tuba) +Cym. (brush)
27
Tempo I
need me a girl in the most aw - ful way. Oh
+Acc.
+Cl.
+Cl. 2
+Snare (brush)
give me a girl ov - er a man an - y day, please
+Stgs
Rit.
pick me a girl, or I'll take one.'
+Tbn. solo
+Acc.
+Vln. (Trem.)
(Pno. out)
+Pno.
+Snare roll
+Vcl.
+Acc. (big)

Tempo
39
Tbn.
40
41
42
ALL:
I
Acc.
Cl. 2
+Cls.
+Cym.
+Low Tom
43
44
45
46
need me a girl in the most aw - ful way. Oh
+Cls.
+Sn. roll
47
48
49
50
give me a girl ov - er a man an - y day, please
+Cr.

V.S.

51
+Cls,Tbn.
52
53
3
54
pick me a girl, or I'll take one.'
+Sn. roll
+Sn. roll
55
56
ALBERTINE:
A
+Acc.
+Stgs. (Trem.)
p
mp
57
58
59
60
man in a bar has cried in - to his beer, he'd
+Cl. 2
+Cl. 1
+Acc.
+Stgs.
+Tbn.

61
62
63
Rit.
64
bet on a horse who had brought up the rear, Now he
+Tbn. (horse whinny)
+Cls,Tbn.
65
Slower
66
67
Rit.
68
comes to my door, and he knocks there three times, and
+Acc.
+Tbn.
69
Slow
70
71
72
this is what I hear him whine: I
+Acc.
+Cym
8vb
loco
Vcl. (pizz.)
V.S.

73
Tempo
74
75
76
need me a girl Oh give me a girl, I
+Cl. 2
+Vln.
+Acc. +Cl. 1
+Tbn,Vcl. (pizz.)
77
78
79
80
need me a girl in the most aw - ful way. Oh
+Snare
81
82
83
84
+Sn. roll
give me a girl ov - er a man an - y day, please
+Cym.
85
Rit.
86
87
3
88
MEN:
(except Marcel)
pick me a girl, or I'll take one.' I
+Cr.
+Vln. (Trem.)
+Sn. roll
+Tbn.
+Cym. roll
+Vcl,Tbn.

Tempo I
ALL:
(except Marcel)
need me a girl Oh give me a girl, I
+Acc.
+Vln.
Vcl,Tbn.
+Sn. roll
+Low Tom
Perc. (sim.)
need me a girl in the most aw - ful way. Oh
+Vln. (Trem.)
give me a girl ov - er a man an - y day, please
+Cr.

V.S.

Rit.
Tempo
101
102
103
104
pick me a girl, or I'll take one.'
Cls,Vln.
Acc.
+Cym.
+Vcl,Cls.
Tbn. Vcl.
105
Rall.
106
ALBERTINE:
A
Cls,Vln.
f
+Sn. roll
107
Tempo
108
109
110
coun - tess a - lone, while her count's out of town, she
mp
Vcl. (pizz.)
+Tbn. (wobbly)

111
112
113
114
Rit.
Tempo
tries out the thea - ter, then tries on a new gown. Now she
+Cls,Tbn,Stgs.
115
Slower
116
117
Rit.
118
comes to my door, and she knocks there three times, and
+Acc.
+Cls.
+Tbn.
+Vcl. (pizz.)
119
Slow
120
121
122
this is what I hear her whine: I
+Vln.
Stgs. (Harm.)
+Vcl. (arco)
8vb
loco
+Tbn.
123
Slower
124
125
126
need me a girl Oh give me a girl, I
+Vln.
+Acc.
8va
+Cls,Vcl.
+Tri.
+Cls,Vcl.
+Cym. scrape
V.S.

Tempo
+Vln.
need me a girl in the most aw - ful way. Oh
+Acc.
+Cl. 1
+Cl. 2
+Vcl.
give me a girl ov - er a man an - y day, please
+Bell of Cym.
+Tbn.
+Tbn.
pick me a girl, or I'll take one.'
Rit.
WOMEN ONLY:
I
+Acc.
(Cls.)
+Vcl,Tbn.
+Sn. roll
Tempo
need me a girl Oh give me a girl, I
ALL:
(except Marcel)
+Vln.
+Acc.
Cl. 2
+Acc.
+Cls.
(Tbn,Vcl.)
+Cr.
+Cym. (light)

143
144
145 +Cls,Tbn,Stgs.
146
need me a girl in the most aw - ful way. Oh
+Vln. (Trem.)
+Sn. roll
147
148
149
150
give me a girl ov - er a man an - y day, please
Cl. 2
+Cr.
151
Rit.
152
pick me a girl, or I'll
+Cym.
V.S.

Allargando
153
take
one.'
154
ALBERTINE:
155
Slower
Please
pick
me
a
+Cls,Acc,Stgs.
f
+Low Tom roll
+Cr.
8vb
Tbn,Acc.
156
(long)
girl,
or
I'll
Grand
157
take
one!!
158
Tutti
+Cls,Acc,Vln.
Tutti
+Cym. scrape
+Tbn,Timp. roll
8vb
Tbn,Acc,Vcl,Timp.

# ACCORDION SOLO

"...and we returned to Paris"

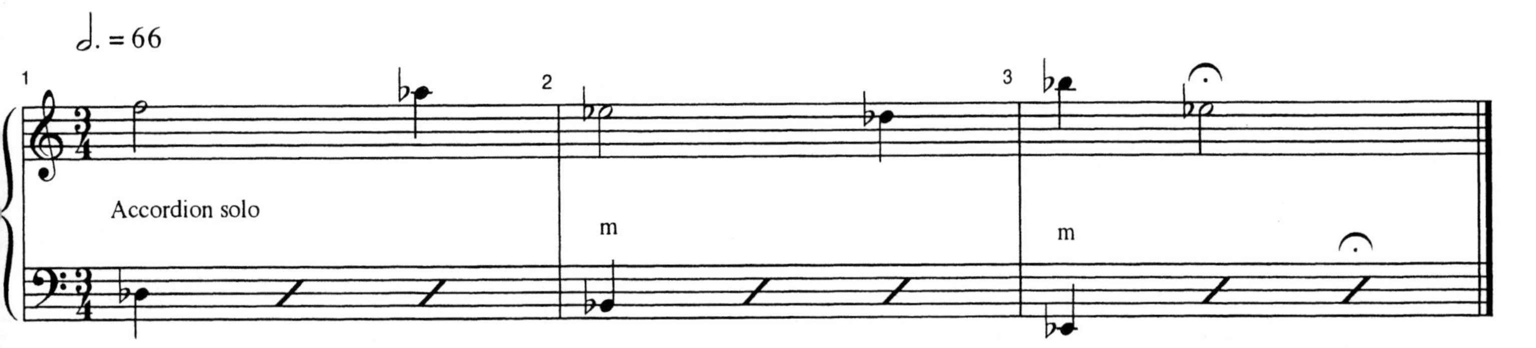

# INCIDENTALS INTO "SOMETIMES"

# SOMETIMES

CUE: "She'll spring upon my bed"
CUE: "Very nice."
Slow, free ♩= 66
Jaunty ♩= 82
+Fl.
mp
+Tbn.
+Cl,Tbn,Acc,Stgs.
Vamp (Vocal last X)
MARCEL:
Some-times I watch her take off her clothes and throw them on a chair. Some - times

Rit.
NARRATOR:
Tempo
Some - times.
Some-times I will put out my light and sit and watch her there. Some - times
(MARCEL)
Some-times
+Fl.
Poco rit.
Tempo
Some - times
Some - times
her hair car-ess - es me so like the wings of a mor - ning dove.
+Fl.
legato
mf
+Fl.
+Fl.
Some - times In - side my mouth is her tongue
+Vibes

18
19
20
now this is what I call true love.
Some - times
+Vln.
+Acc.
+Fl.
8va
Cl,Vcl.
+Mark Tree gliss.
21
22
23
Some-times I un-but - ton her che-mise be-fore I go to bed. Some - times
loco
f
mp
+Fl,Cl,Acc,Vln.
+Cym. (brush)
24
25
26
Some - times
Some-times I kiss her lit-tle breasts un-til I am well fed
Some - times
8va
15ma
loco
+Bells
mf
loco
+Tbn,Vcl,Cym. (brush)

27
28
29
Some - times
Some - times
Some - times
Some-times I touch the hol - low
+Fl,Cl.
+Bells
8va
+Vln. (pizz.)
+Fl,Cl.
30
31
32
Some - times
that lies be-tween the thighs. Some - times
Some - times
+Vln. (pizz.)
8va
loco
+Vibes
+Acc.
+Vcl.
+Vln.
+Fl,Cl.
33
34
35
Some-times she'll o - pen wide the door I'll hear the hing - es sigh. Some -
Some -
+Mark Tree
+Vcl.
+Vln,Acc.
+Stgs. (Trem.)
+Cl,Tbn.
Tbn.
+Cym. (brush)

Poco rit.
times Some - times Some - times
times Some - times Some - times
+Fl.
8va
+Acc.
loco
+Stgs.
+Cym. roll
Cl,Stgs.
8vb
39
Tempo
Very elastic
Some - times I touch and watch as two white legs like swans necks bend
+Cl,Tbn,Acc,Stgs.
+Fl.
mp
+Cl,Stgs.
Rit.
Slower
Rit.
Oh Some - times Some - times
Oh some - times Some - times Some - times
+Fl.
+Bells
15ma
8va
loco
Fl.
8va
+Cl.
Stgs. (Trem.)
f
+Vcl.
8vb

Rit.
Some - times they push up hard and then back down a -
Fl. solo
+Cl.
mp
+Acc.
+Stgs.
+Vcl.
+Cl,Vcl.
+Cym.
8vb
Rit.
Free
Faster
gain.
Some - times
Some -
+Vln.
+Acc.
+Fl,Cl.
sub. f
+Tbn.
+Vln.
loco
+Tbn,Acc,Vcl,Timp. roll
Accel.
times
Fl,Cl,Vln. (Trill)
tr
port.
+Vcl
+Sus Cym.
accel.
Cl,Tbn,Acc,Stgs.
Applause Segue

# BUT WHAT I SAY IS...
# (REPRISE)

MARCEL: Love
NARR.:
MARCEL:
NARR.:
BOTH:
NARR.:
Need me, want me. Want me. And what I want is Love me, love me.
loco
+Fl.
+Bells
+Vln.
+Acc.
+Vcl.
+Fl,Cl.
Vcl.
+Cl.
me.
Rit.
Tempo
BOTH:
But what I think is
Please have me.
+Fl,Cl.
+Acc.
Stgs. (Trem.)
+Vln.
+Vln.
+Tbn.
+Tbn,Vcl.
Rit.
Slower
ALBERTINE:
But all I say is
MARCEL:
Please take me. Taste all of me! But what I know is
NARRATOR:
Please take me. Taste all of me! But what I see is
+Fl.
+Fl.
+Cl.
+Vcl.
+Tbn,Acc,Vln.
+Tbn.
+Cym. roll

21
Tempo
22
no - thing. No - thing. No - thing. What I say is
no - thing. No - thing. No - thing. What I say is
no - thing. No - thing. No - thing. What I say is
+Fl.
3
23
24
Rit.
no - thing. No - thing. No - thing.
no - thing. No - thing. No - thing.
no - thing. No - thing. No - thing.
+Bells
f

25
Tempo
26
Poco rit.
27
Tempo
Where is she go - ing? Is what I think.
To take a bath?
+Fl.
mp
sub. p
3
+Sus Cym.
28
29
Molto rit.
30
But all I say is
Is what I think. But all I say is
But all I say is
f
(Vcl.)
+Fl ,Vln,Acc. (Trem.),Cl. (Trill)

Tempo
Rit.

31 32

no - thing. No - thing. No - thing.

no - thing. No - thing. No - thing.

no - thing. No - thing. No - thing.

+Fl.

+Tbn,Cl,Acc,Stgs.

+Cym. scrape

Colla voce (slow)

33 34 35

Un - til all I think is

Un - til all I think is

8va

**Almost segue**

# SOMETIMES (REPRISE)

cue: Our worst fears.

7
8
Some - times I will put out the lights and sit and
Sop.
+Tbn,Vcl. (pizz.)
9
10
Rit.
watch her there Some - times Some - times Some - times
+Sxs.
+Tbn.
+Vcl.
+Sus Cym.
11
Tempo
12
her hair ca - res - ses me so like the wing of a mor -
legato
mf
Tbn,Vcl.
13
14
Some - times
ning dove
+Vln. (trem.)
Alto (cued)
+Acc.
+Tbn,Vcl.

P/V/C
3. SOMETIMES (REPRISE)
My Life With Albertine
in - side my mouth is her tongue
Now this is what I call true
+Alto,Vln.
+Sop.
Sxs,Tbn,Vln.
+Tbn.
+Vcl.
love
8va
+Vln. (trem.)
+Acc,Sus Cym.
SOLO:
Some - times I un - but - ton her che - mise be - fore we
f
+Vcl.
Vcl.
go to bed
SOLO:
Some - times
SOLO:
Some - times
SOLO:
Some - times
+Vln.
8va
15ma
+Sus Cym.
- 143 -

SOLO:
Some - times I kiss her lit - tle breasts un - til I am well fed
+Sxs,Tbn.
decresc.
SOLO:
Some - times Some - times Some - times
+Vln (pizz.),Acc.
SOLO:
Some - times I touch the hol - low that lies be - tween the
+Sxs,Tbn,Vln.
Rit.
Colla voce
+Tri.
Tempo
thighs Some - times Some - times Some - times
Vln,Acc.
Tbn.
+Alto
+Sus Cym.
+Sop.

31
32
Some-times I o - pen wide the door I'll hear the
Sxs,Acc.
+Vln.
f
Tbn.
+Vcl,Acc.
33
+Vln.
34
Rit.
hing - es sigh Some - times Some - times Some -
Alto,Tbn.
cresc.
+WB
+Sop,Acc.
+Cym. (Bell)
8vb
Tempo
35
36
times
8va
ff
(8vb)
37
Tempo
38
Some - times I touch and watch as two white legs like
Vln.
+Alto
+Sop.
sub. mp
+Vln. (pizz.)
Tbn,Vcl. (pizz.)
+HH (16ths)

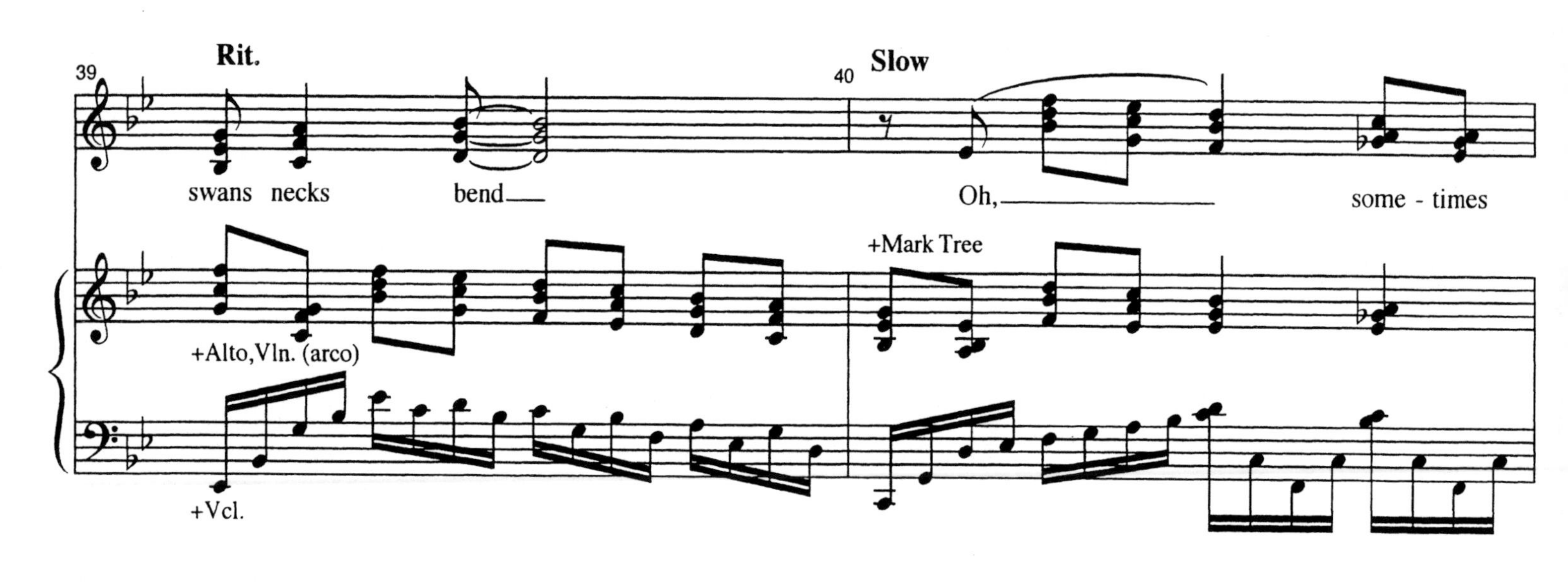
39
Rit.
swans necks bend
40
Slow
Oh,
some - times
+Mark Tree
+Alto,Vln. (arco)
+Vcl.

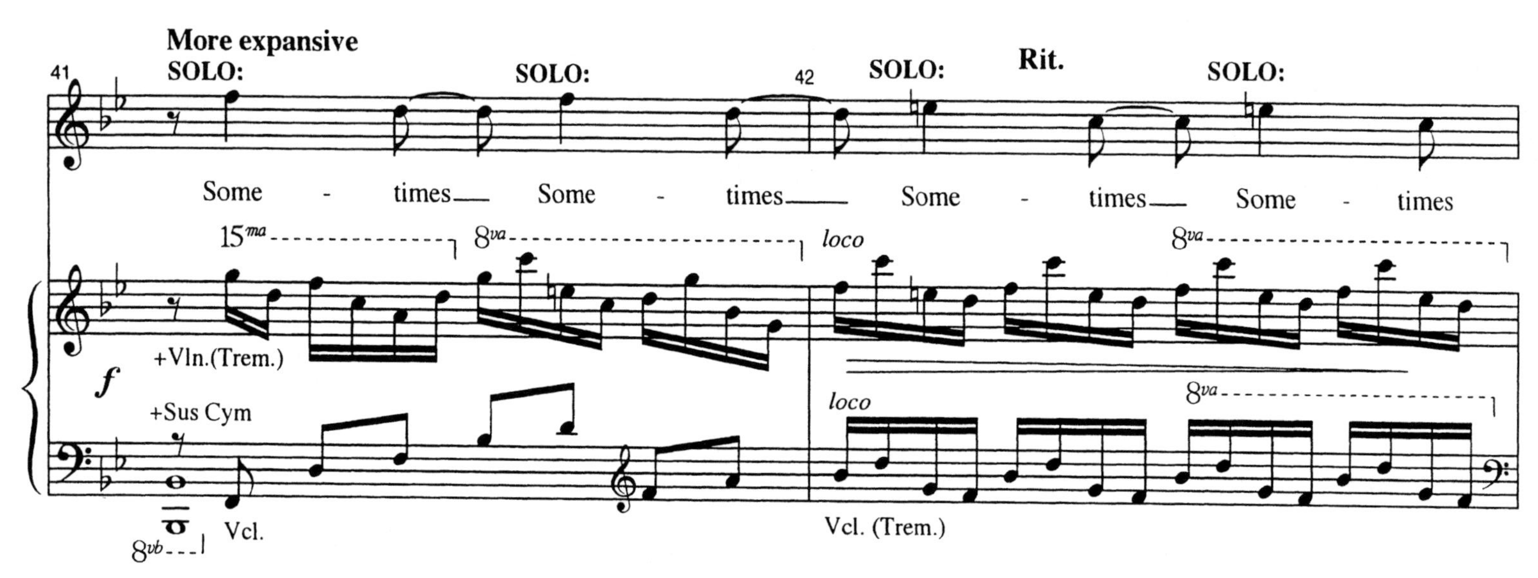
41
More expansive
SOLO:
Some - times
SOLO:
Some - times
42
SOLO:
Rit.
Some - times
SOLO:
Some - times
15ma
8va
loco
8va
+Vln.(Trem.)
f
+Sus Cym
loco
8va
8vb
Vcl.
Vcl. (Trem.)

43
Slower
Some - times they push up
44
hard
Rit.
and then back
Sop.
+Alto
mp
+Acc.
+Tbn. (plunger growl)
+Vcl.
+Sus Cym.

Tempo (slow)
down a - gain.
Rit.
Alto solo
+Sop.
+Vcl.
8vb
+Vln.
+Tbn. (open)
Freely
Tempo
Some - times
Some - times.
f
+Sxs,Vln. (Trem.)
+Cr.
+Low Tom roll
Acc.
+Sxs,Vln.
+Vcl.
tr
+Cr.
Sxs,Tbn,Acc,Vcl.

This page left blank intentionally for page turns

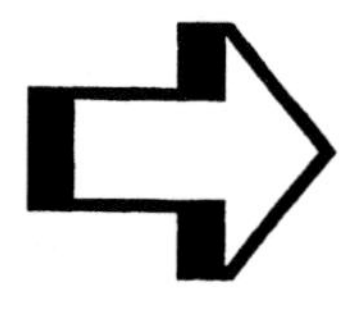

# FERRET SONG REPRISE (PART 1)

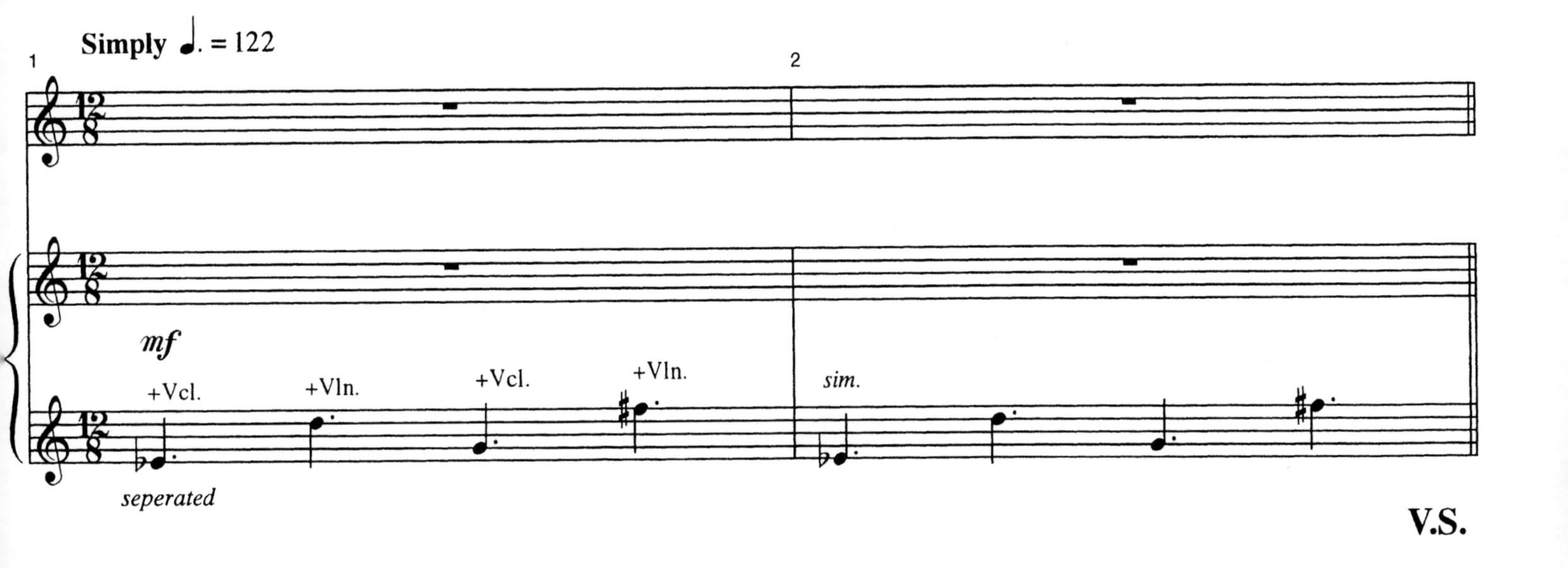

3
ALBERTINE: (half singing, half humming)
Oh Fer-ret of Fai-ry wood he just ran by
Oh Fer ret of Fai ry wood he passed by me
+Cl.
(Stgs. sim.)
La La La La La La La La La La La La La La La La La La La La
mp (underscore)
Stgs.
(Pno. LH cue only)
La La La La La La La La La La La La La La La La La La La La
La La La La la La La La La La La
La La La La La La La La La La La
(Pno. plays)

Safety (vocal last time)
17 MARCEL:
18 ALBERTINE:
19 MARCEL:
Rit.
20 ALBERTINE:
Oh Fer-ret of Fai-ry wood
Whom will I mar-ry?
Oh Fer-ret of Fai-ry wood
whom will I love?
+Fl.
+Cl.
(Pno. LH cue only)
21 Tempo
22
23
24
(to 27)
+Fl.
+Stgs. (pizz.)
+Acc, Stgs. (arco)
(Pno. plays)
27
28
29
30
+Stgs. (pizz.)(as before)
(Pno. LH cue only)
31
32
33
34
Vln. (arco)
Vcl. (arco)

Cue: "She's in the bath." [Andree goes behind the screen...]
Vamp (on cue: rit. & continue)
Simply ♩ = 96
Vln. (arco)
mp (underscore)
+Acc.
Vcl. (pizz.)
(Pno. plays)
8va
loco
+Stgs.
+Acc.
Acc,Vln.

# FERRET SONG REPRISE
# (PART 2)

CUE: that could have just been a dream

12
Safety
13
14
15
CUE: STOP on "I'll come with you"
+Acc.
Stgs. (sim.)
(Pno. out)
16
17
18
19
(Pno. plays)
20
21
Acc.
+Cl.
+Fl.
+Vln.
+Vcl.
22
23
24
25
+Stgs. (pizz.)

26
27
28
29
+Fl. (cued in Acc.)
30
31
32
33
+Fl.
34
35
36
37
38
39
40
41
+Cl.
+Fl.
+Stgs. (pizz.)
+Acc.
+Acc.

This page left blank intentionally for page turns

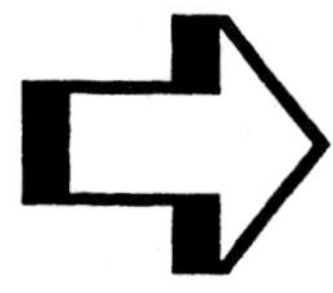

# FERRET SONG REPRISE (PART 3)

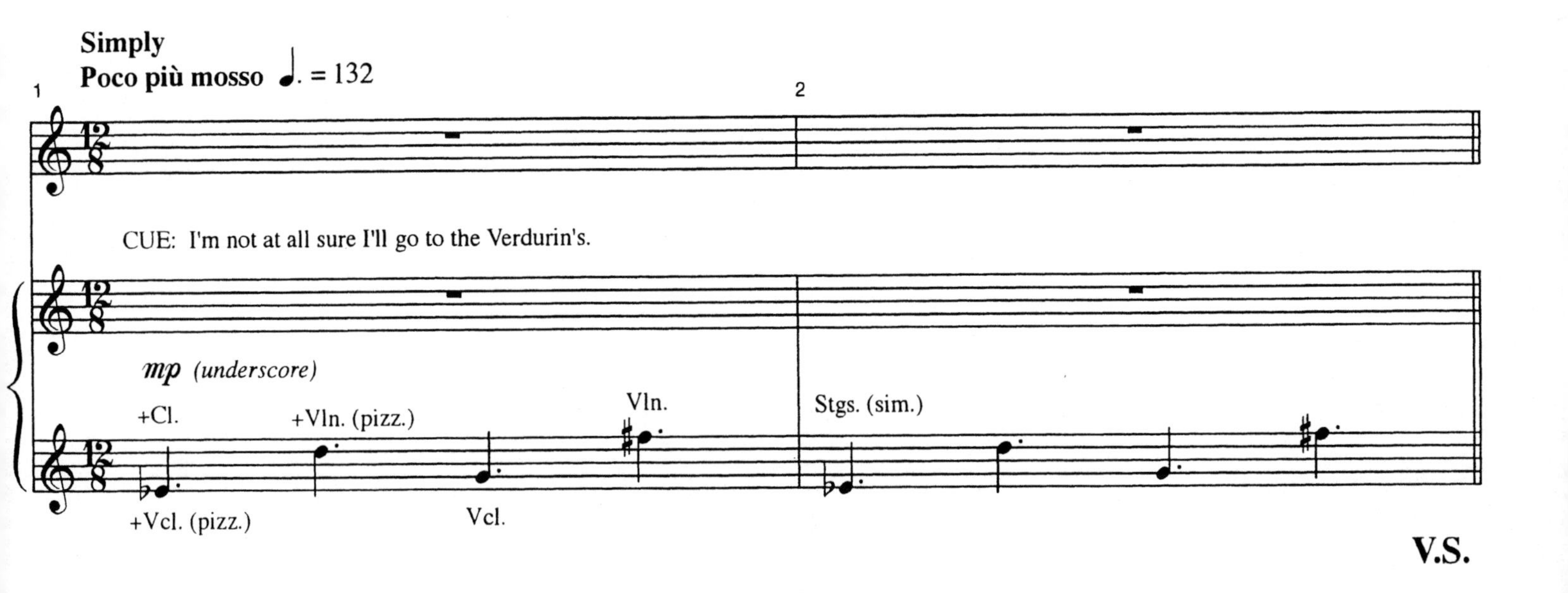


V.S.

3
Safety
4
5
6
STOP on word: But she asked me to go buy it BEFORE
+Acc.
(Pno. out)
7
8
9
10
11
12
Acc.
+Cl.
+Vcl.
+Fl.
13
14
15
16
+Stgs. (pizz.)

17
18
19
20
+Fl. (cued in Acc.)
21
22
23
24
+Fl.
+Acc.
+Acc.
25
26
27
28
+Stgs. (pizz.)
29
30
31
32
+Cl.
+Fl.
+Stgs.
+Acc.
+Acc.

# FERRET SONG REPRISE
# (PART 4)

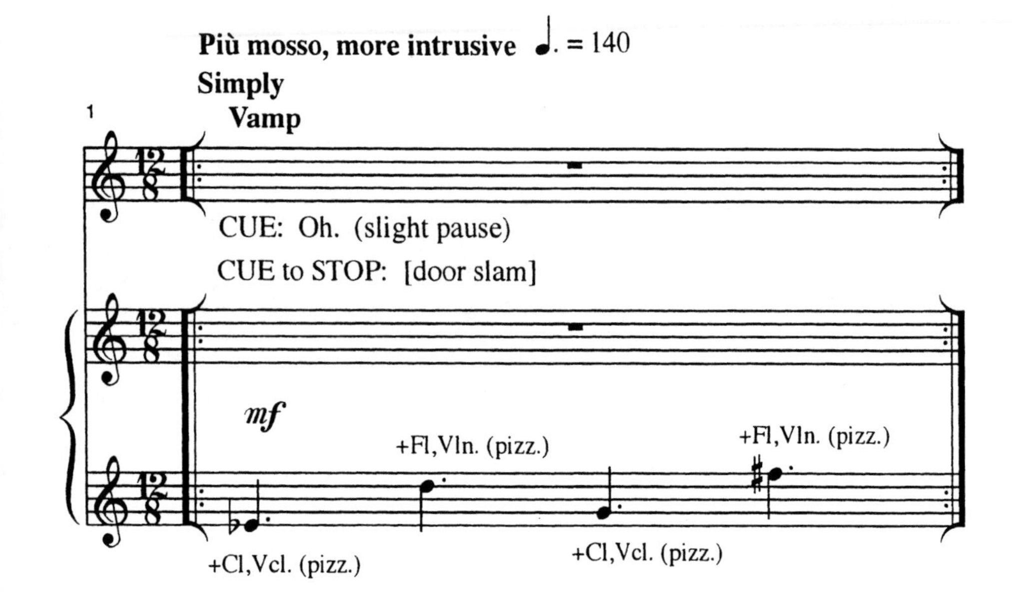

# THE STREET

Cue:"Albertine?"

+Fl.
Tin. Tin. Tin. Tin - ker here.
+Fl.
Tin. Tin. Tin. Tin - ker here.
+Anvil
+Xylo
+Acc. (LH)
+Vcl.
+Tbn.
WOMAN:
Snails by the pail snails cheap and snails for sale!
Snails by the pail snails cheap and snails for sale!
+Vln.
+Acc.
mf
+Cl.
+Tbn,Vcl.
+Fl.
f
+Ratchet
2nd WOMAN:
Pe - ri - win - kles Mol - lusks Ask us.
Pe - ri - win - kles Mol - lusks Ask us.
+Fl.
6
+Vln.
+Fl.
Vcl.
+Cl,Acc,Vcl.
+WB
3rd MAN:
Knives, scis - sors shar - pened
Knives, scis - sors shar - pened
f
+Cl,Acc,Vcl.
+Vibes

19
3rd MAN:
+Fl.
20
Ra - zors too. Ra - zors
Ra - zors too. Ra - zors
(Cl,Vln.)
+Fl.
+Cl,Vln.
+Vcl.
+Vcl.
21
3rd WOMAN:
22
Rags! Rags! Rags!
Rags! Rags! Rags!
+Bell Tree
23
4th WOMAN:
Poco rit.
24
Dogs clipped cats wormed tails cut.
Dogs clipped cats wormed tails cut.
8vb

* "Ah's" should be like car horns or fog horns yearning.

29
1st MAN:
30
Al - ber - tine
Al - ber - tine
Tin. Tin. Tin. Tin-ker here.
Tin. Tin. Tin. Tin-ker here.
Ah
Ah
Ah
Ah
Ah
Ah
Ah
Ah
Ah
Ah
Cl,Acc,Vln.
+Fl.
+Anvil
+Fl.
+Anvil
+Xylo
sim.
+Tbn.Vcl.
+Cym. scrape

31
MAN:
32
Al - ber-tine Al - ber-tine
Al - ber-tine Al - ber-tine
WOMAN:
Ah Ah
2nd WOMAN:
Ah Ah
3rd MAN:
Ah Ah
3rd WOMAN:
Ah Ah
4th WOMAN:
Ah Ah
+Fl.
+Xylo
+Fl.
+Vcl.
+Tbn.

33
MAN:
34
Al - ber - tine
Al - ber - tine
2nd MAN:
Al - ber - tine
Al - ber - tine
WOMAN:
Snails by the pail snails cheap and snails for sale!
Al - ber - tine
2nd WOMAN:
Ah
Ah
3rd MAN:
Ah
Ah
3rd WOMAN:
Ah
Ah
4th WOMAN:
Ah
Ah
+Vln.
+Acc.
mf
+Cl.
+Tbn, Vcl.
+Fl.
+Ratchet
f
+Cl, Tbn.
+Ratchet

35
36
Al - ber-tine Al - ber-tine
Al - ber-tine Al - ber-tine
WOMAN:
Al - ber-tine Al - ber-tine
Pe - ri - win - kles Mol-lusks Ask us. Al - ber-tine
Ah Ah
Ah Ah
Ah Ah
+Fl.
6
+Cl,Vcl.
+WB
+Vln.
+Fl.
+Cl,Vcl.

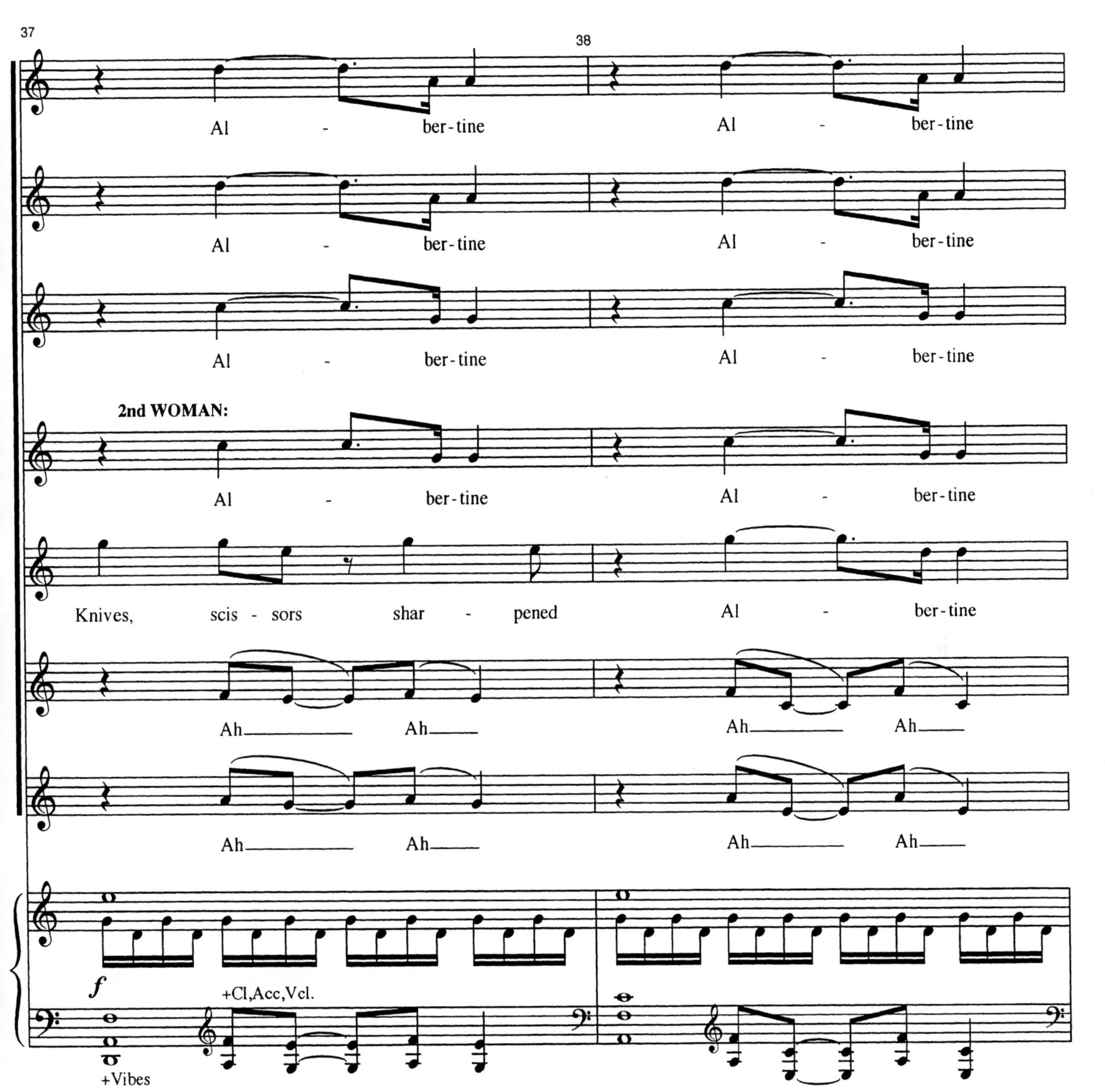
37
38
Al - ber-tine Al - ber-tine
Al - ber-tine Al - ber-tine
Al - ber-tine Al - ber-tine
2nd WOMAN:
Al - ber-tine Al - ber-tine
Knives, scis - sors shar - pened Al - ber-tine
Ah Ah Ah Ah
Ah Ah Ah Ah
f
+Cl,Acc,Vcl.
+Vibes

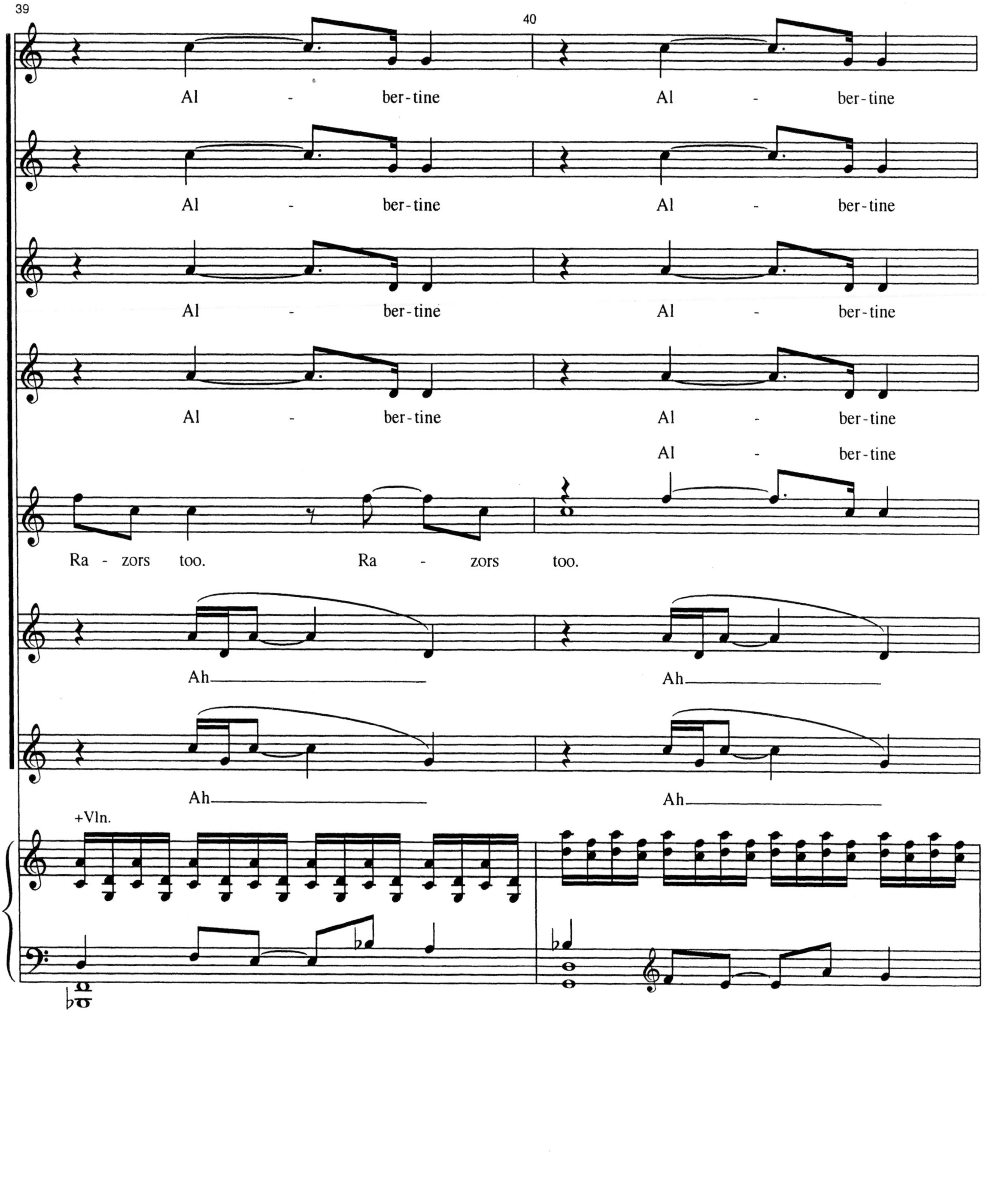

39 40

Al - ber-tine Al - ber-tine

Al - ber-tine Al - ber-tine

Al - ber-tine Al - ber-tine

Al - ber-tine Al - ber-tine

Al - ber-tine

Ra - zors too. Ra - zors too.

Ah Ah

Ah Ah

+Vln.

41
42
Al - ber-tine Al - ber-tine
Al - ber-tine Al - ber-tine
Al - ber-tine Al - ber-tine
Al - ber-tine Al - ber-tine
3rd MAN:
Al - ber-tine Al - ber-tine
Rags! Rags! Rags! Al - ber-tine
Ah Ah
ff
+Vcl.
+Tbn.

* Who ever sings highest
(and MARCEL)

46 **Anxious** ♩ = 96

47 48

think I hear her foot - steps Think I see her skip - ping

+Fl,Cl,Acc,Stgs.

*mf* +Tbn.

8vb

Poco rit.
A tempo
Think I see her so hap - py just be - ing a -
+Fl.
decresc.
mp
8vb
way from here.
a - way from here.
+Fl.
Rit.
A tempo
+Tbn,Vcl.
+Fl,Vln.
+Vln. (Trem.)
cresc.
+Sus Cym.
ff
+Tbn,Vcl.
loco
Rit.
A tempo
Rit.
= 69
+Vln.
ALL:
a - way from here.
A - way from here Al - ber - tine
+Acc,Stgs.
+Tbn.
(Pno. solo)
f
+Cym. scrape
+Vcl.

65
Rit.
66
MARCEL:
67
(he closes window)
Al - ber-tine
Al - ber-tine
(instr.)
(Pno. solo)
mp
+Acc.
(Vcl.)

# SAD BALBEC #2 (A)

# SAD BALBEC #2 (B)

# SAD BALBEC #2 (C)

CUE: (2nd x this line is said): "That danger has been averted" (bell)

# SAD BALBEC #2 (D)

This page left blank intentionally for page turns

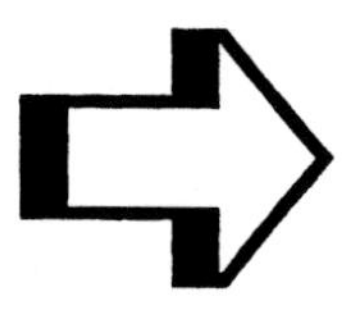

# THE DIFFERENT ALBERTINES (REPRISE)

Play solo softly as underscore, follow dialogue cues. Band in at m.36.

Cue:"My dear Albertine, it is better that we part." [narrator sits at piano and begins to play]

11
12
("no hurry")
13
14
(Pno. solo)
15
Safety
16
17
18
("...unhappy...")
1st x only
8vb
19
20
Rit.
21
Tempo
22
Rit.
8vb
("Fine.")
23
accel.
24
Rit.
cresc.

Rit.
("Ask.")
(Pno. solo)
cresc.
8vb
Tempo
Safety
Cue to continue:
"You're crying."
Rit.
Tempo (slower)
f
mf
mp
Rit.
"...see this room again."
Slowly
("Now I'll be unhappy!")

Espressivo (flexible) (♩ = 108)
37
Rit.
NARRATOR:
Al - ber - tine...
+Cl,Bs Cl,Acc,Stgs.
Cl,Vln.
mp
+Cym.
Tempo
Rit.
Al - ber - tine...
Tempo
A
+Cl,Vln.
+Vcl.
+Cl,Acc,Vcl.
Rit.
Tempo
Rit.
sil - hou - ette a - gainst the sea, and ev - 'ry - time I look I see a diff - 'rent
+Cl. 1
+Vln.
+Euph.
cresc.
+Cym. roll
(Vcl.)
+Euph.
Tempo
Rit.
Al - ber - tine, Al - ber - tine
Cls,Vln.
mf

Underscoring
♩ = 80
grazioso
Cls.
mp
Vcl.
8va
+Euph.
+Vln.
+Vcl.
+Acc. solo
V.S.

60
61
62
63
Rit.
+Vln.
cresc.
+Vcl. (pizz.)
Safety
Tempo (♩ = 92)
1st x only
Cue to continue: "Do you love me even a little bit?""More than ever."
64
65
66
67
Rit.
1st x only
+Cl,Bs Cl,Vln. (1st x only)
f
+Vcl. (1st x only)
68
69
+Cls,Vln.
8va
mp
+Euph,Vcl.
+Bells
70
71
72
Vln.
+Vcl.

Molto rit.
Tempo
Rit.
Tempo
+Cl.
+Vcl.
Rit.
+Vln.
cresc.
+Vcl. (pizz.)
Safety
Tempo
1st x only
rit. and continue on cue:
("Of my love?")
Cl,Acc,Vln. (1st x only)
+Tam-tam (1st x only)

Meno mosso
("...sat next to her...")
("...curve...")
("then withdrew...")
+Cl.
Rit.
+Vln.
+Vcl.
Tempo
Rall.
Tempo, expansive
Rit.
Oh
+Cl. 2,Euph.
+Vln. (Trem.)
+Vcl. (Trem.)
+Acc.
+Euph.
Tempo
Rit.
Tempo
Rit.
Al - ber-tine.
Oh
Al - ber-tine.
Oh
+Cls,Vln.
+Cls,Vln.
+Vcl.
Rit.
Tempo
MARCEL &
NARRATOR:
Al - ber - tine.
A
Cls.
+Vcl.
+Acc. (cued in Vln.)

Rit.
(MARCEL on top)
sil - hou - ette a - gainst the sea,
and ev - 'ry - time I look I
+Acc. (cued in Vln.)
cresc.
+Cls,Vln.
+Vcl.
+Euph.
♩ = 100
see
a diff - 'rent...
mf
Vcl. (Trem.)
+Acc. (soli)
+Sus Cym.
+Cls,Vln.
+Euph.
+Vcl.
Vcl. (Trem.)
Acc.
Rit.
+Euph.
Slower
MARCEL:
Rall.
Slower
Oh
Al - ber - tine.
+Cls,Vln.
sub. mp
p
mp
+Euph.

117
Slower
NARRATOR:
118
119
Rit.
120
121
Slow
122
Each time I look I see a diff - 'rent
+Cl,Acc. (cued in Vln.)
pp
+Vcl.
+Timp. roll
ppp
+Bs Cl,Vln.
Safety [continue after bell rings]
123
♩ = 100
124
125
126
girl.
1st x only
Vln,Acc.
Last x only
p
+Vcl.
+Sus Cym.
+Bells
+Cl.
127
Poco accel.
128
129
130
131
("Mlle. Albertine is gone.")
132
+Vln. (Trem.)
(Cl,Acc,Vln.)
+Bell Tree
Tutti
p
+Vcl.
+Euph.
poco cresc.
(Bs Cl,Vcl.)
mf
+Sus Cym.
Bs Cl.
Acc.
+Sus Cym.
8vb
Almost segue

# THE LETTERS

Cue: "She left a letter with me for Monsieur."
Espressivo ♩= 104
Rit.
(to 9)
Solo Piano
mp legato
+Cym.(brush)
8va
+Cl.
loco
+Triangle
ALBERTINE:
Dear one I am gone we have reached the end bet - ter to leave as friends be -
+Vln.
+Fl.
+Vcl.(cued in Acc.)
fore we hate and hurt each o - ther more. I leave you I leave you I
+Pno.
+Fl,Cl.
cresc.
+Acc.
f
+Euph.
+Sus Cym.

(Pno.)
leave you I leave you my best part, my heart.
(Fl,Cl,Acc,Vln.)
decresc.
mp
(Vcl.)
(Euph.)
+Fl.
+Fl,Cl,Acc.
+Euph.
Rit.
Tempo
ANDREE:
Mocking (♩ = 116)
Al - ber-tine. I leave you I leave you I
+Vln.
loco
mf
+Fl,Cl.
sim.
+Vcl.
+Cym.(scrape)
+Euph.
+Acc,Vcl.
leave you I leave you my best part, my
+Cl.
(Vcl.)
(Euph,Vcl.)
Rit.
(To 35)
heart. Al - ber - tine.
mp
+Cl.
+Bells

Tempo
35
FRANCOISE:
Ma - dem - oi - selle Al - ber - tine is gone!
+Vln.
+Fl,Cl.
(Vln.)
(Fl,Cl,Acc.)
+Cl.
(Acc,Euph,Vcl.)
+Cym.(scrape)
+Vln.
Poco rit.
+Fl.
(Acc.)
+Cl.
+Vln.
sub. mp
+Vcl.
+Cl.
Tempo
43
NARRATOR:
+Fl.
My cle - ver friend I write you now com - mend - ing your wis - dom
+Vln.
+Vcl.(cued in Acc.)
You, with your smart and watch-ful eyes, saw through my thoughts, ex - posed my lies.
+Cl,Vln.
cresc.
+Acc.
+Euph.
+Sus Cym.

+MARCEL:
+Pno.
MARCEL: and
So fare-well
So fare-well
So fare-well
So fare-well
(Cl,Euph,Acc.)
+Vln.
+Fl,Cl.
+Fl.
f
+Vcl.
go to hell.
NARRATOR: Go to hell.
Mar - cel.
GIRLS:
I
mp
+Fl,Cl,Acc.
+Vcl.
+Acc.
+Euph.
58
GIRLS:
leave you I leave you I leave you I leave you my
MESSENGER:
So fare-well So fare-well So fare-well So fare-well and
(Vln.)
+Fl,Cl.
mf
+Vln.
(Acc.)
(Vcl.)
+Acc,Vcl.

Rit.
best part, my heart. Al - ber-tine.
2nd MESSENGER JOINS:
go to hell. Mar - cel.
(Fl,Vln.)
(Cl.)
(Fl.)
8va
+Bells
(Euph,Vcl.)
(Cl,Acc,Stgs.)
Tempo
2nd MESSENGER:
Ma-dem-oi-selle Al - ber-tine there's more
loco
+Fl,Cl.
(Vln.)
(Bells)
(Acc.)
f
(Euph.)
+Vcl.
GIRLS:
Dear one I am gone we have reached the end bet-ter to
2nd MESSENGER:
My cle-ver friend I write you now com-mend-ing your wis-dom
MARCEL & NARRATOR:
+Fl. Yes, we'll not meet a-gain I will not
+Vln.
+Cl,Vcl.
+Euph.
+Cl,Vcl.

73
WOMEN:
74
75
76
leave as friends be - fore we hurt and hate each o - ther more. I
MESSENGERS:
You, with your smart and watch-ful eyes, saw through my thoughts, ex-posed my lies.
M. & N.:
friend.
think of you as lov - er or as lov - er or as friend,
(Fl.)
(Acc,Vln.)
cresc.
(Fl,Cl.)
+Bells
f
+Euph,Vcl.
+Cl.(Vcl.)
+Euph.
+Cl,Vcl.
+Euph.
+Cl,Vcl.
77
78
79
80
leave you I leave you I leave you I leave you my
So fare-well So fare-well So fare-well So fare-well and
un-til the last coal of our dead love's cold and ash - en and my
+Bells
+Vln.
+Fl.
+Cl,Vln.
+Fl.
+Cl,Vln.
+Fl.
+Cl,Vln.
+Fl.
+Cl.
(Acc.)

81
82
83
84
Rit.
best part, my heart.
go to hell.
Go to hell.
Go to hell
Go to hell
black glove waves fare - well Go to hell. Go to
(Fl.)
(Vln.)
(Fl,Cl,Acc,Vln.)
(Acc.)
+Vcl.
+Cl,Euph.
+Vcl.
+Cl,Euph.
+Timp.
+Euph.
+Vcl.
Tempo (Maestoso)
85
FRANCOISE:
86
87
Rit.
88
Ma-dem - oi - selle Al - ber-tine is gone!
+Vibes
+Fl,Cl,Vln.
(Cl.)
+Vcl.
(Acc,Euph.)
f
(Stgs.)

Poco più lento ♩= 108
ALBERTINE:
Dear - est one you must know that I love you still and that my love will ne - ver die,
no, no mat - ter whom I'm with. So know I kiss you I kiss you I kiss you I kiss you
E - ven when it's a - no - ther I kiss. Al - ber - tine.
GIRLS:
I kiss you I
(Vibes)
+Cl,Vln,Acc.
+Vcl.
(Euph.)
+Fl.
+Cl.
(Vcl.)
+Vln.
+Acc.
+Euph.
Rit.
Tempo
+Sus Cym.
+Fl,Cl.
+Vibes
loco
+Cl.
+Fl,Cl,Stgs.
(Acc.)

105
106
107
kiss you I kiss you I kiss you
(Fl,Cl,Stgs.)
(Acc.)
(Euph.)
108
109
110
E - ven when it's a - no - ther
E - ven when it's a - no - ther
E - ven when it's a - no -
+Vibes
+Fl,Cl.
3
(Euph.)

Rit.
Tempo
– I kiss. Al - ber - tine.
– I kiss. Al - ber - tine.
ther I kiss. Al - ber - tine.
(Fl,Cl.)
loco
(Vln.)
+Fl,Cl,Vln,Bells
(Acc.)
(Vibes)
(Euph.)
+Sus Cym.
(Vcl.)
ALBERTINE:
Ma-dem-oi-selle Al - ber - tine is gone! (hold thru dialogue)
"What are you writting?"
Al - ber-tine is gone
GIRLS:
FRANCOISE:
Ma-dem-oi-selle Al - ber-tine is gone!
+Fl,Vln.
+Acc.
+Vibes
+Cl.
Tempo
MARCEL:
My dear-est "A", I write you just to say (and please don't faint)
(Fl,Cl,Vln.)
(Fl.)
+Drs.(HH)
(Acc.)
(Euph, Vcl.)

+NARRATOR:
Rit.
121
122
123
124
I'm get-ting mar-ried a - ny day,
her name? You won't be - lieve,
An-dree.
(Fl,Cl,Vln.)
+Cl.
+Fl.
(Acc,Drs.)
(Euph, Vcl.)
Tempo
BOTH:
125
126
127
128
Rit.
I want you I want you I want you I want you
(Fl,Cl,Stgs.)
(Euph.)
+Vibes
GIRLS:
Poco meno mosso
129
+Fl.
130
131
132
fin - 'lly to see me hap - py at last.
Stay well.
Mar- cel. I
+Fl.
(Acc,Vln,Euph,Vibes)
+Cl,Vcl.
+Cl,Vcl.
(Acc.)

133
Più mosso
GIRLS:
134
135
kiss you I kiss you I kiss you I
3 MESSENGERS:
I want you I want you I want you
(Fl,Cl,Stgs.)
8va
(Acc.)
(Euph, Acc.)
CHORUS OF WOMEN:
136
137
138
139
Molto rit.
kiss you E-ven when it's a-no - ther
E - ven when it's a-no - ther
E-ven when it's a-no -
CHORUS OF MEN:
I want you fin-'lly to see me hap - py
fin - 'lly to see me hap - py
fin-'lly to see me hap -
loco
+Vibes
+Fl,Cl.
3

**Slower**

140 141 142

_ I kiss Al - ber-tine.

_ I kiss Al - ber-tine.

ther I kiss Al - ber-tine.

_ at last Stay well. Mar - cel.

_ at last Stay well. Mar - cel.

py at last Stay well. Mar - cel.

+Fl,Cl. 8va +Sus Cym. loco +Cl,Vln. 8va +Fl,Cl.

3 f ff (Acc.)

(Vcl.)

(Euph, Acc.) (Vcl.)

Tempo
147
GIRLS W/ALBERTINE:
148
149
150
Dear-est one you must know that I love you still and that my love will ne-ver die,
MESSENGERS W/MARCEL & NARR.
My dear-est "A", I write you just to say (and please don't faint) I'm get-ting-
(Fl,Cl,Vln.)
8va
(Acc.)
loco
mf
(Vcl.)
(Euph.)
+LoTT
+SD(Acc.)
8vb loco
(Euph.)
151
152
153
Rit.
154
Tempo
– no, no mat-ter whom I'm with. So know I kiss you I
mar-ried a-ny day, her name? You won't be - lieve, An-dree. I want you
+Fl.
FRANCOISE:
Ma-dem-oi-selle Al -
(Fl,Cl,Stgs.)
f
(Acc.)
+Concert TT's
+Sus Cym.
(Euph.)

155
156
157
158
want you I miss you I need you I leave you I
I kiss you I need you I miss you I hate you
ber-tine is gone!
Ma-dem-oi-selle Al -
(Fl,Cl,Stgs.)
+Cym.(crash)
(Acc,TT's)
cresc.
+Euph.
(Euph.)
8vb
159
160
161
Allargando
Slower (♩ = 80)
162 MARCEL:
love you I hate you
Stop!
"Stop this. Stop. That's enough."
I love you I leave you
ber-tine is gone!
+Cl.
sub. mp
8vb
+Sus Cym.
Cym.(choke)

163
164
165
166
167
+Pno. 8va ten.
+Acc. 3
+Vcl.(mute)
+Vln.(mute)
+Pno.
168
♩ = 88
169
170
171
3
(Acc.)
mp
+Vln.
+Vibes
(Vcl.)
+Cl.
+Pno.
172
173
174
Rit.
175
3
(Acc.)
(Vcl.) 3
+Vibes
espr.
+Pno.
Slightly Faster, tenderly
Vamp
176
177
Continue on: "...our
Albertine is no more."
178
Rit. (last x)
179
180
"...but she died."
+Stgs.
+Vln.
legato
+Vibes
(Acc.)
+Vcl.
(Vibes)
Segue

# ALBERTINE'S LAST LETTER (REPRISE - NARRATOR)

Cue: Begins to open it.

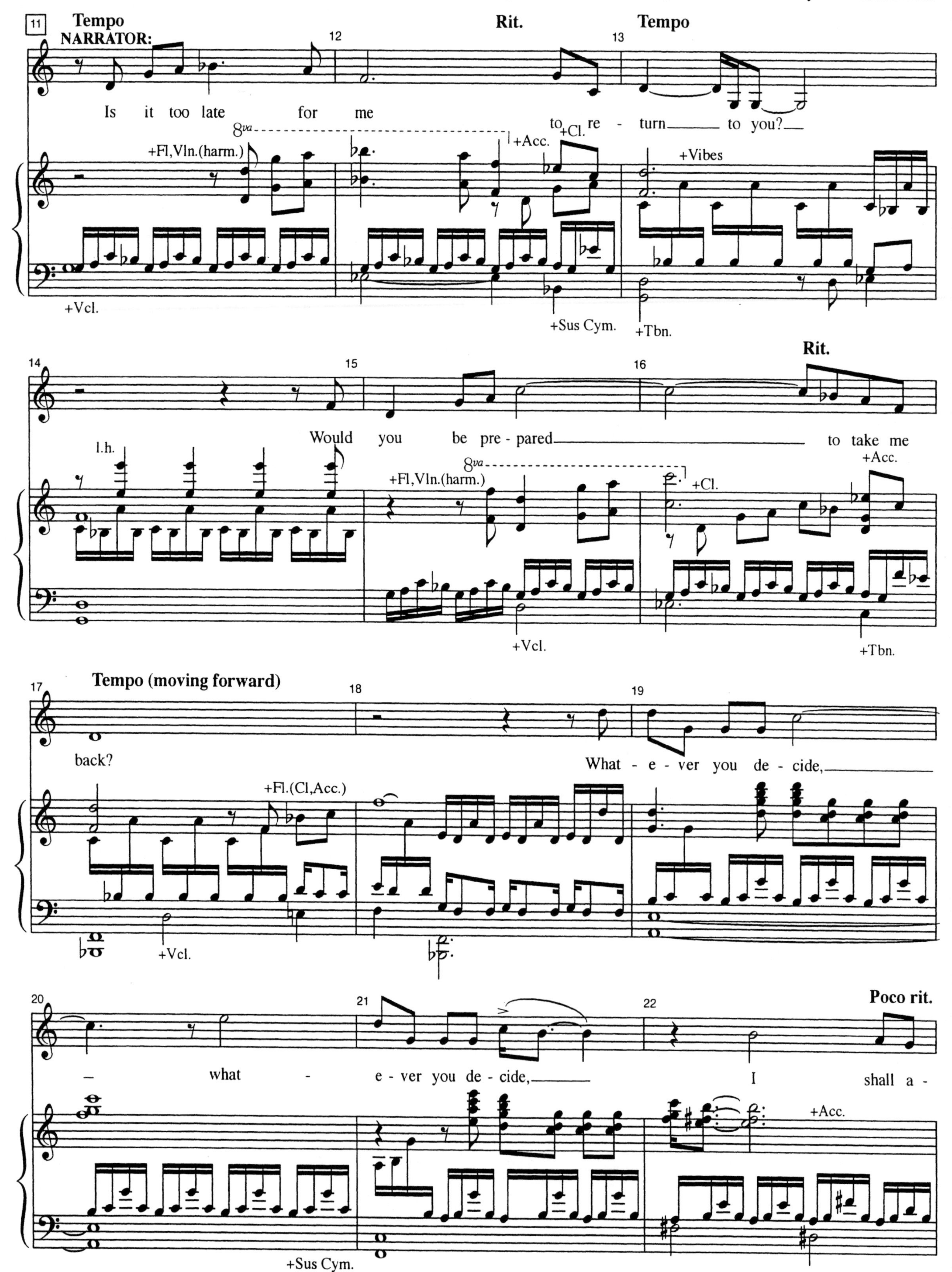
Tempo
NARRATOR:
Rit.
Tempo
Is it too late for me to return to you?
8va
+Fl,Vln.(harm.)
+Acc.
+Cl.
+Vibes
+Vcl.
+Sus Cym.
+Tbn.
Rit.
Would you be pre-pared to take me
l.h.
8va
+Fl,Vln.(harm.)
+Acc.
+Cl.
+Vcl.
+Tbn.
Tempo (moving forward)
back?
What-e-ver you de-cide,
+Fl.(Cl,Acc.)
+Vcl.
what-e-ver you de-cide,
Poco rit.
I shall a-
+Acc.
+Sus Cym.

23
24
Rit.
25
Tempo
bide
by your de - ci - sion.
(Acc.)
+Vln.
+Fl,Cl.
+Stgs,Triangle
(Vcl.)
26
Poco accel.
Rit.
27
Tempo
28
Rit.
+Fl,Vln.(harm.)
+Cl.
+Acc.
+Tbn.
+Vcl.
+Tbn.
29
Tempo (poco più mosso)
30
Rit.
31
Tempo
If you know now, I
+Vibes
+Vln.(trem.)
8va
+Fl,Vln.(harm.)
+Vcl.
32
Rit.
33
Tempo
34
beg, please, don't make me wait.
The
(8va)
loco
+Cl.
+Acc.
+Vibes
l.h.
+Tbn.

Rit.
Tempo (moving forward)
ink from your pen will seal my fate.
+Fl,Vln.(harm.)
+Cl.
+Cl,Acc.
+Vcl.
Acc,Tbn.
+Sus Cym.
(Vcl.)
What - e - ver you de - cide,
what
+Fl.
+Vibes
(Fl,Pno.)
+Sus Cym.
+Tbn.
Rit.
Tempo
e - ver you de - cide,
what
e - ver you de - cide,
(Fl,Cl,Vln.)
loco
(Cl.)
+Fl.
+Acc,Tbn.
Poco accel.
Poco rit.
I shall a - bide by your de - ci - sion.
+Cl.
+Vln.(trem.)
sub. p
+Tbn.
mp

47
Più mosso (anxious)
accel. poco a poco
+Vln.
Im - pa-tient-ly wai - ting.
48
+Vln.
In - sa-tia-bly long - ing
(Cl.)
mf
accel. poco a poco
(Vcl.)
49
Poco accel.
I shall board the
+Fl,Vln.
Bells
8va
+Tbn.
50
train at once
+Cl.
+Fl,Vln.
+Vcl.
51
Rit.
if you say to me
+Fl.
+Acc.
+Sus Cym.
52
Maestoso
"re - turn."
+Cl.
(Vcl.)
+Timp.
53
Rit.
Oh, I
(Fl.)
(Vcl.)
(Cl.)
+Sus Cym.
+Tbn.

54
Tempo (meno mosso)
burn to know...
+Fl, Vln.(harm.)
+Acc.
mp
(Vcl.)
55
Rit.
I
+Cl.
+Fl.
56
Tempo (più mosso)
yearn to know
+Vibes
+Tbn.
57
(Fl, Vln.)
l.h.
58
Rit.
My whole heart is
l.h.
59
A Tempo
ach - ing.
(Cl, Acc, Vln.)
(Vcl.)
60
Rit.
My whole heart is
+Vibes(Fl.)
l.h.
61
A Tempo
yours.
(Cl, Acc, Vln.)
(Vcl.)
+Tbn.

Più mosso
+Fl.
+Vln.
Poco rit.
Your
Al - ber-tine.
(Acc.)
cresc.
(Vcl.)
+Tbn.
8vb
+Timp.
+Sus Cym
Tempo
(Fl,Cl.)
Broadening
Your
Al - ber-tine.
(Fl,Cl.)
+Bells
(cresc.)
(Tbn.)
More deliberate
Rit.
Oh
+Fl,Vln.
+Acc.
+Cl.
(Acc.)
f
(Vcl.)
(Tbn.)
Tempo
Rit.
Al - ber-tine.
+Vln.
(Cl,Tbn. cued)
+Vibes
pp
+Acc.
(Vcl.)
+Timp.

This page left blank intentionally for page turns

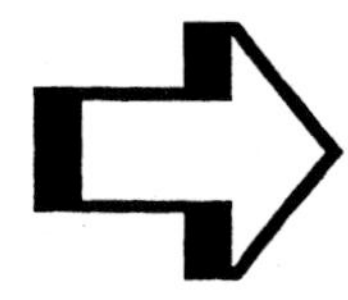

# IF IT IS TRUE

Cue. "Albertine?"
Simple, sweet ♩ = 100
mp legato
+Vln.
+Vcl.
+BsCl.(cued in Euph.)
+Fl,Bells
ALBERTINE:
If it is true, if it is so, you love me.
+Acc.
+Fl,Bells

13
14
15
16
If it is true, and I have heard you
+Acc.
(Vln.)
(Vcl.)
(BsCl.)
17
18
19
20
do. Then
+Fl.
+Bells
(Acc.)
21
22
23
24
Rit.
I am weal - thi - er than a king with
8va
+Fl,Bells
+Pno.
Tempo
25
26
27
28
Rit.
love of you.
(Acc.)
+Fl,Bells
+Cl.
+Euph.
+Vcl.
+Sus Cym.

29
Tempo, fuller
30
31
32
If it is so, if it is
+Fl,Cl,Stgs.
mf
+Euph.
+Vcl.
8vb
33
34
35
36
true, you love me.
+Fl,Acc.
+Cym.(brush)
(Cym.)
37
38
39
40
Rit.
If when at night dream - ing you
(Acc.)
+Vln.
+Cl.
+Vcl,Euph.
41
Tempo
42
43
44
dream of me. Then
+Bells
+Fl.
+Cl.

45
46
47
48
Rit.
I am luck - i - er than the king who
+Fl,Cl.
Vln.
+Acc.
8vb
Tempo
49
50
51
52
Rit.
rules the sea.
And
+Cl.
+Vln.(pizz)
+Fl.
Vln.(arco)
+Cym.(brush)
(Cym.)
+Sus Cym.
53
Tempo (poco più mosso)
54
55
56
if I die a sud - den death for
+Vln.
+Cl.
+Fl.
mp
+Euph.
57
58
59
Rit.
60
rea - sons why I do not know.
But
+Pno.
+Sus Cym.

Tempo
Molto rit.
if I die a sud - den death to
(Acc.) +Fl.
Fl.(solo)
mp
(Stgs.)
+Pno.
+Cl.
(Euph.)
Tempo I
accel. poco a poco
live for - e - ver in par - a - dise...
Fl,Bells
pp
+Cl.
accel. poco a poco
+Vln.
+Vcl.
Accel.
+Fl.
mp
cresc.
+Cl,Vln.
+Euph,Vcl.
+Sus Cym.
+Acc.
I will not be as hap - py
+Fl.(8va)
mf
+Euph.

77
+Bells
78
79
80
in all that time, as I have
(Fl.8va)
+Vln.
+Cl,Acc.
(Euph.)
81
82
83
84
been with you..
+Fl.(8va)
+Bells
cresc.
85
accel. poco a poco
86
87
Rit.
88
Fl.(solo)
3
+Cl,Vln.
+Cl.
accel. poco a poco
+Euph.
+Vcl.
+Sus Cym.

89
Very broadly
+Stgs.
90
91
92
If it is true, if it is so, you
Bells
f
+Cl.
93
Più mosso
94
95
96
love me.
Fl,Cl.
+Bells
mf
+Vcl.
97
Rit.
98
99
Allargando
+Fl.
100
If it is true, and I have heard you
+Vln.
(Acc.)
+Cl.
(FL.)
+Cl.
mp
f
+Euph.

Tempo
do.
Then
+Vln.
+Fl.
+Cl.
mf
+Vcl.
mp
(Euph.)
+Euph.
I am weal - thi - er than a queen with
Rit.
+Acc.
+Fl.
mf
mp
A tempo
love of you.
Rit.
8va
+Cl,Acc.
+Fl,Bells
+Vcl.
+Euph.
Slower
I am weal - thi - er than a king with
8va
p
+Triangle
8vb

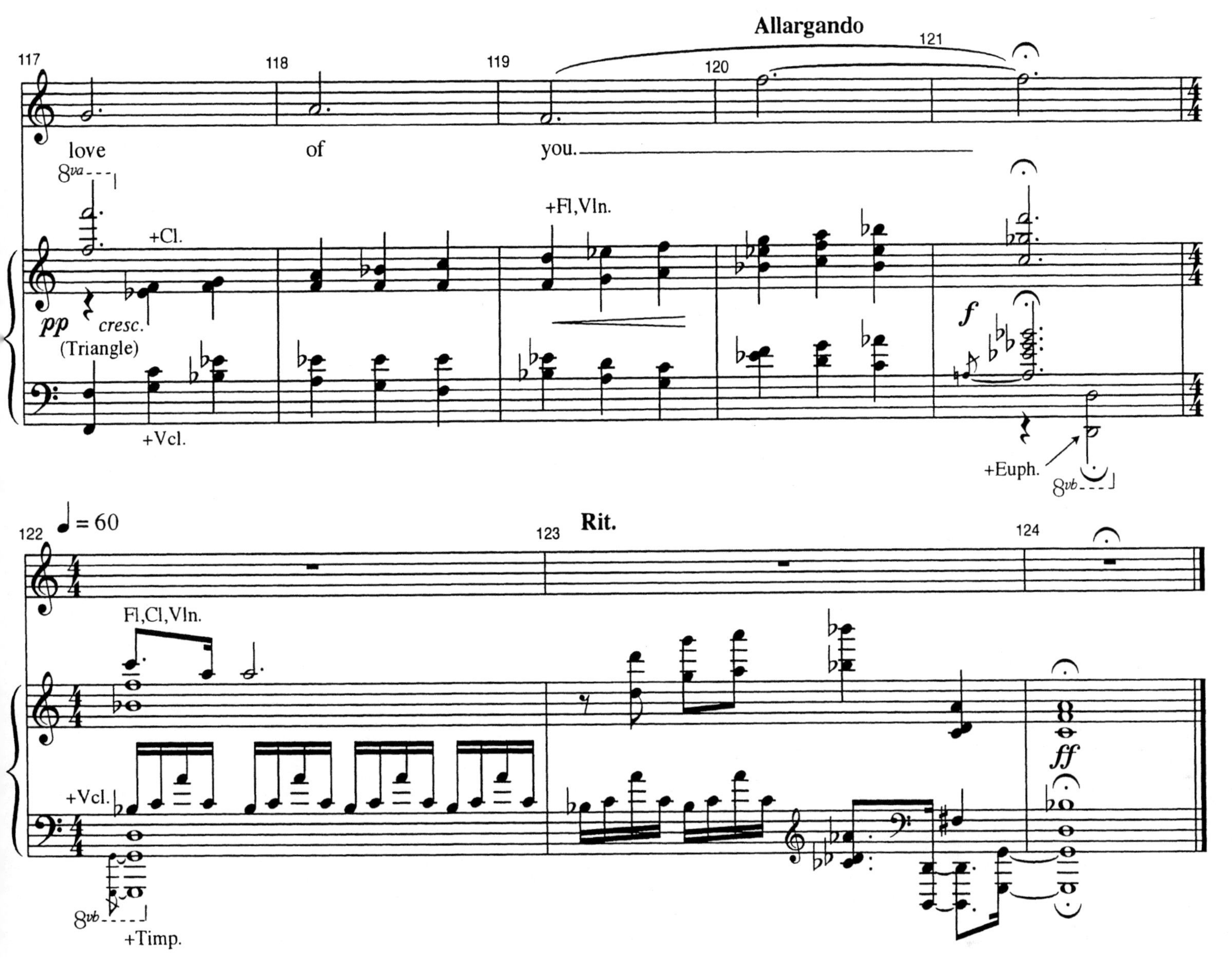
Allargando
love
of
you.
8va
+Cl.
pp
cresc.
(Triangle)
+Vcl.
+Fl,Vln.
f
+Euph.
8vb
♩= 60
Rit.
Fl,Cl,Vln.
+Vcl.
8vb
+Timp.
ff

# BOWS
# ("My Life With Albertine")

# EXIT MUSIC

V.S.

Maestoso (slower)
Vln.(trem.)
Vln.(loco)
Tempo
(Sop,Cl,Acc.)
Pno.
8va
loco
Acc.
f
(Tbn.)
+Vcl.
+Vcl.(pizz)
+Slapstick
Rit.
(Sop,Cl.)
(Pno.(solo)
+Vcl.
+Acc.
+Tbn.
+Timp.
accel. poco a poco
Stgs.
(trem.)
mp
cresc.
+Sus Cym.
+Tbn,Vcl,
Timp.
8vb
loco
+Sus Cym.
Tempo
Acc,Vln.(8va)
(Sop,Cl.)
+Sus Cym.
+Xylo.
Vln.(loco)
+Tbn.
+Vcl.

Slower
Sop,Acc.
Rit.
Vln.
8va
+Cl.
loco
mf
+Tbn,Vcl.
+S.D.
Tempo
Slower
Rit.
Acc.
+Vln.
+Sop.
(Rit.)
+Vcl.
+W.B.
+Tbn.
+Sus Cym.
Broadly
Deliberate
+Xylo.
Cl,Sop.
Acc,Vln.
+Vcl.
+Tbn,
Timp.
Presto
Vln.(trem.)
Sop,Cl,Acc.
+Tbn,Vcl.
sfz
+Sus Cym.
+Timp.